The POCKET GUIDE TO

Woodstock

From the authors of *Walking Woodstock: Journeys into
the Wild Heart of America's Most Famous Small Town*

Michael Perkins & Will Nixon

❖ ❖ ❖

❖ ❖ ❖

BUSHWHACK BOOKS | WOODSTOCK, NY

The Pocket Guide to Woodstock.
Copyright © 2012 by Michael Perkins & Will Nixon.

Contact the publisher for information.

Printed in the United States of America.

Book cover and interior design by Joe Tantillo.
Cover and interior illustrations by Carol Zaloom

ISBN 978-0-615-65216-0

Library of Congress Cataloging-in-Publication Data
The Pocket Guide to Woodstock / Michael Perkins & Will Nixon.
[Woodstock, NY] : Bushwhack Books, 2012.

    197 p. ; ill. : cm.

ISBN 978-0-615-65216-0
1. Woodstock (N.Y.)—History. 2. Walking—New York (State)
—Ulster County—Guidebooks.
974.734
F129   .W85

Bushwhack Books
Woodstock, New York

www.bushwhackbooks.com
USA 845-679-5853

To Alf Evers (1905-2004)

The Woodstock Historian
Who Inspired Many of Us

❖   ❖   ❖

Table of Contents

Welcome to Woodstock

You are about to explore a small town with a large hold on the world's imagination because of a landmark rock festival that didn't happen here. By all reports, Woodstock itself was a ghost town that weekend in August, 1969, when upwards of half-a-million young people converged on a dairy farm 60 miles across the Catskills in Bethel, New York. That "Woodstock" has been memorialized in movies, books, and two more festivals (which also didn't happen here). So how did this little village of white churches and cozy boutiques grab all the glory? How did Woodstock become the most famous small town in the world?

In truth, Michael Lang, the festival's young producer, who'd recently moved here from Florida where he'd run a head shop and staged the Miami Pop Festival, didn't try very hard to hold his Woodstock festival in town. Touring the area, he hadn't seen a site big enough for his ambitions. The town fathers also had made it clear they didn't want a hippie invasion. So the location was set for Wallkill, 40 miles south of Woodstock, until that town voted them out a month before the concert date. Only then did Lang discover the bucolic setting that he'd envisioned from the start, a natural amphitheater in rolling pasture lands. On a handshake deal, he secured use of Max Yasgur's dairy farm. The rest is rock 'n' roll history, now made tourist-friendly at the Bethel Woods Center for the Arts, where graying Baby Boomers can relax in lawn chairs while listening to Crosby, Stills & Nash.

Yet Lang never wavered in naming his event after Woodstock. He'd found a spirit here that he wanted to share with the world. You could say that he tapped into traditions that dated back to Woodstock's origins as an arts colony in 1902. One evening after his arrival he went to a Sound-Out, a casual farm field concert where nationally acclaimed musicians jammed on the back of a flat bed truck. This series was in its second summer and could perhaps be traced back to folk festivals held in town in the late 1950's and early 1960's—or, if you really wanted to go back in history, the Maverick Festivals of the 1920's at which people dressed up in gypsy costumes that in vintage photos make them look like Jazz Age versions of hippies and flower children. So that night, as Lang lay on his picnic blanket under the stars listening to some great blues, history was in the air. So was the scent of marijuana and a communal vibe. People had brought sleeping bags and set up lean-tos beside their VW vans. Enchanted, Lang had his Big Idea. Why not do a bigger version of a Sound-Out, one with Jimi Hendrix, his star attraction at the Miami Pop Festival?

Today, Woodstock may seem like a tie-dye time warp where Jimi Hendrix and Bob Marley rule like saints in the tee shirt shops. On summer weekends Father Woodstock himself, an eternal hippie in peace buttons and robes but not unlike Uncle Sam, may greet you on the Village Green. But as you explore, you, too, will notice the arts colony legacy that infuses village life to this day. It's in the galleries and crafts shops. It's in the historic white buildings that once were boarding houses or homes. It's in the busy summer events calendars jammed with too many choices: a photography workshop or a chamber music concert, an art gallery opening or an author reading, a summer stock musical or outdoor Shakespeare—performed perhaps with a motorcycle on stage. From May through October, the Woodstock Arts Consortium of almost a dozen organizations coordinates openings on Second Saturdays of the month, providing a cultural bonanza.

Now that Woodstock is famous for one festival, why stop? The Woodstock Poetry Festival convened three times in the early 2000's to present such luminaries as Lawrence Ferlinghetti and Robert Bly, Billy Collins and Sharon Olds. Since 2000, the Woodstock Film Festival has grown into a major event each September, spilling over into Rhinebeck and Rosendale. Billing itself as "fiercely independent," it screens dozens of films at various locations. Some may be duds, such as one shot in town starring Jane Fonda as a hackneyed hippie grandmother growing pot in her basement, but many are great discoveries. Now there's a Woodstock Writers Festival in the spring. The famous white dove perched on a guitar neck in the 1969 festival poster has returned as a white owl perched on a yellow pencil.

If you'd like to walk the hallowed grounds of the 1969 festival, by all means visit the Bethel Woods Center for the Arts. But if you'd like to be where it got started, you've come to the right place. A week before Hendrix was helicoptered out to Bethel to close the festival, he jammed at the Tinker Street Cinema here in town for an audience of about 50. If you say you were there, surely you're lying. But you can be there now. You're in Woodstock, the most famous small town in the world.

The Woodstocker

People who live in Woodstock have always been considered a trifle odd by their neighbors in surrounding areas. Citizens of Kingston are recorded as looking askance at Woodstockers for their eccentricity and contentiousness as early as the late 18th century. Beginning with the arrival of visitors to Woodstock's summer boarding houses in the late 19th century, a connection to New York City has shaped the outlook of its residents. After the establishment of Byrdcliffe in 1902 and the resulting influx of art students, tolerance for diversity became perhaps the most important aspect of a distinctive Woodstock personality.

Woodstock's mix of natives, proud of their heritage, and artists, affluent weekenders, and full-time resident newcomers has created the Woodstocker: kind, generous, tolerant, intelligent, individualistic, opinionated, cosmopolitan, and community-minded.

A good cause can always find support here, whether it is local or international. Nothing unites Woodstockers like tragedy—raffles are set up to help victims, and benefit concerts are sold out. Ulster County's premier private social service agency, Family of Woodstock, was founded to aid stranded hippies who came here because of the 1969 festival, and today it offers a full range of services to the needy.

Woodstockers are blasé about the presence of celebrities in their midst. When Paul Newman sat on a bench on the Village Green one afternoon, he was allowed to enjoy the passing scene like anyone else. When Muddy Waters and Bob Dylan held photo sessions on Tinker Street, it was ho-hum. The famous have always found refuge here.

Woodstock has a vibrant volunteer spirit. After the Woodstock Playhouse was destroyed by arson, a private group was formed that succeeded in bringing it back. People happily volunteer to help out fire and ambulance services, run arts organizations, serve on town committees, and work at any number of community events. Each August the town holds a Volunteers' Day picnic followed by evening fireworks, a celebration to thank the more than 1,000 people who help over 40 local organizations.

Woodstockers are opinionated. From battles within arts organizations to political *contretemps*, highly intelligent people take principled stands. Just attend a town board meeting or watch one on the local cable channel to see self-appointed community watchdogs get hot under the collar over any number of issues. Woodstockers care passionately about their town and about protecting the natural environment.

Or read *Woodstock Times*, which has held a mirror up to Woodstock life for 40 years. This independent weekly showcases the talents of an extraordinary community with columns on politics, culture, gardening, the outdoors, and astronomy. For a taste of local concerns—and contentiousness, check out its latest Letters to the Editor.

Woodstockers are fond of doing bloody battle over what outsiders might consider trifles. That politicians say nasty things about each other is to be expected; but when a local arts organization wouldn't renew the lease of a popular restaurant a war broke out: headlines, picketing, mass meetings that engaged the attention of Woodstockers for over a year. Eventually, the restaurant moved across the street and did better business than before.

This tempest in a teapot phenomenon pops up every few years, especially at the local arts organizations. Some blame this negative side of Woodstock on a population of overeducated people with too much time on their hands. Others whisper darkly about a "curse." (Legend has it that the Native Americans wouldn't live in the valley because they thought it was haunted by evil spirits.) Some ugliness has been more serious. In the past Woodstock had its share of anti-Semitic incidents. A majority of noodle-headed artists slavishly followed the Stalinist party line. It's difficult to remain starry eyed about Woodstock if you've lived here long enough. Yet we stay, loyal to our friends and the beautiful surroundings, convinced our town is like no other, even in its outbreaks of nastiness.

Stop a Woodstock resident walking down Tinker Street and you're likely to find an internationally famous attorney, publisher, composer, novelist, artist, musician, poet, actor, or banjo player. This resident likely supports cultural events, attends the town's legendary parties, argues burning issues in the local newspapers, is probably a liberal of some stripe in a conservative county, and will stubbornly Stand on Conviction.

A Brief History

Stand on the Woodstock Village Green and close your eyes. Tune out the traffic noises. Let your imagination time-travel back through Woodstock history. If it is a summer day, the Green will be crowded. Open your eyes now and see the people around you as characters from Woodstock's past. You will see Native Americans, Dutch and English settlers, Revolutionary War militia, farmers, loggers, tanners, glass workers, sawmill workers, witches, actors, artists, writers, and world-famous celebrities. If you can view Woodstock through the lens of your imagination, you will become part of this gathering. Step into history....

Woodstock was incorporated in 1787, but people have been coming here for over 4,000 years. The first were the Algonkian-speaking Esopus people, who lived on the banks of the Esopus Creek and visited Woodstock to hunt and fish. They called the area "Waghkonk" — "place at or near a mountain." Their greatest legacy is all around us. By setting fires, they replaced the original forest of beech and maple trees with open, park-like woodlands that grew nut-bearing trees that fed both game animals and themselves: oaks, hickories, chestnuts, and walnuts. The oak forest they brought to Woodstock still covers our hills and valleys today.

Johannes Hardenbergh began buying land from Esopus sachems in 1705, amassing a "Patent" of a million and a half acres in the Catskills. By 1762 a large portion of the Patent was held by Robert Livingston of Clermont, across the Hudson River. Livingston and his descendants owned Woodstock until the mid-19th century, leasing land to settlers for the duration of three lifetimes. (At one point, a woman—a Livingston—was the town's landlady.) But Livingston agents had trouble collecting rents: citizens dressed as "Calico Indians" protested in the Down Rent War of 1844, and the Livingston family lost its hold on the land.

During the Revolutionary War, patriots and Tories (residents loyal to the king) skirmished here. Two Woodstockers were taken as prisoners by the British to Canada. The great Mohawk leader Joseph Brant was active on the Tory side.

The valley towns of Kingston, Hurley, and

Marbletown had been settled in the 1660's, but it was not until the 1790's and 1800's that many people moved west into Woodstock. No longer European immigrants, they were second, third, and fourth generation Hudson Valley farmers. The local Dutch spoke a dialect that people from Holland wouldn't have understood. The Lutheran Church founded in Woodstock in 1806 was probably the first Lutheran Church in America to prepare its documents in English rather than German.

These families planted crops and cleared pastures for sheep and cows, but the forests drove the economy. For the first half of the 19th Century glass factories along the upper Sawkill in Shady were the major industry in town, brought here by the fuel wood available for furnaces. Sawmills came and went along the streams. The tanneries on Tannery Brook had a long run, grinding up tree bark stripped from hemlocks for the tannins. The bluestone quarries that had at first produced stones for local chimneys and floors began sending sidewalk slabs to New York City.

The 1855 state census reported 1806 residents in Woodstock, including 31 African-Americans. Tinker Street was a dirt road.

In winter and spring, snow and mud made it difficult to travel. People stayed home, or they gathered around the stove in the general store on the Green, or in the barrooms of the two large hotels. Because of the tanneries on the Tannery Brook, the town often stank.

After the Civil War Woodstock began drawing visitors. Tourism replaced the glass factories and, eventually, the tanneries and bluestone quarries. Each summer, the natural beauty and cool breezes brought city residents to stay at the Overlook Mountain House or in the many boarding houses of the area. New Yorkers typically took a boat up the Hudson, boarded a train in Kingston (the abandoned tracks still run alongside Route 28), got off at West Hurley, and took a wagon to Woodstock up Route 375. Most visitors still arrive by this road, with the same breathtaking views before them.

At the turn of the 20th century, the artists arrived, brought by the founding of the Byrdcliffe Arts Colony and the establishment of the summer school of New York's Art Students' League. In the 1920's the town flourished with summer stock theater, chamber music, and Maverick Festivals under full moons in August. The civic minded founded the library, golf club, and chamber of commerce. In 1956 IBM opened in Ulster, adding to the mix of summer artists and local families a professional class that changed parts of town into a commuters' suburb. In the 1960's the rock and rollers arrived, leading to the 1969 festival, followed by the hippie invasion and a great bar scene with legendary live music. As the Baby Boomers have aged, the village has grown more upscale and sedate. Weekenders now own more than half of the houses, changing the ambiance and the real estate prices. The tie-dye tee shirt shops may suggest that Woodstock has gotten stuck in its past. Not so. New people bring new ideas.

What's next is anybody's guess.

Use your imagination.

❖ ❖ ❖

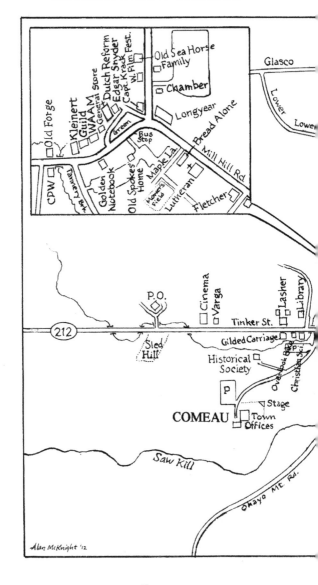

Alan McKnight '12

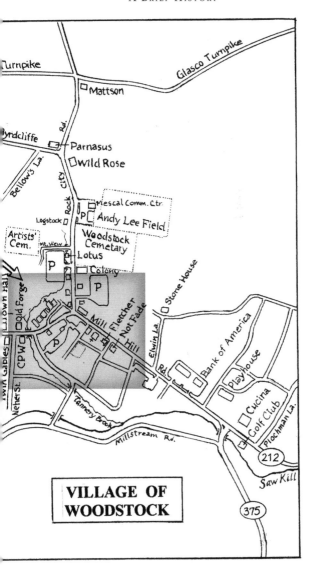

VILLAGE OF WOODSTOCK

A Walking Tour of the Village

The Village Green

Begin your walking tour of Woodstock at the Village Green. It is the hamlet's living room, just a stone's throw from the site of Woodstock's first house built in 1777 by a settler named Newkerk. Here musicians of varying abilities spontaneously drum, strum, and sing for the passing public, and teenagers court and cavort. Here the Trailways bus deposits visitors from around the world. As a public stage open to all, it has been the scene of many political demonstrations. The fondly remembered Woodstock Market

Fairs were held here from World War I to the 1970's. Not so fondly remembered were the local constables who met hippies stepping off the bus in the 1960's to send them back home. In recent years the Green was covered with stonework. The flower gardens in summer are magnificent.

Every Christmas Eve, Woodstockers gather in festive numbers to greet Santa's arrival after dark, a tradition that dates back to 1932. How will he enter town this time? By camel or elephant, as in the early days? Or by flying Volkswagen bus or jet powered sleigh, as in recent years? It's always a surprise.

In the last decade Halloween has brought out a giant gallimaufry of zombies, witches, and goblins. So far, Woodstock has been spared the limping onslaught of the Zombie Crawls that have invaded nearby Saugerties and Rosendale.

Older Woodstockers still recall autumn cider pressings on the Green. Members of the Balmer clan, led by colorful patriarch Ed Balmer, brought an antique cider press to make fresh cider for everyone—a real link with the town's rural past.

To mark United Nations International

Peace Day in September 2008 a red cedar **Peace Pole** was unveiled with the phrase "May Peace Prevail on Earth" translated into 100 languages. The peace symbol atop this Babel of words could just as well be the Woodstock town seal since it shows up everywhere: store signs, windows, tee shirts. We've even seen it scratched by skaters on pond ice and raked into a leaf pile on a front lawn. Every December it appears as a large wreath of blue lights on a house at the edge of town.

Tinker Street

(Walking west from the Village Green)

Organized in 1799, the first small **Dutch Reformed Church** (16 Tinker Street) was built off the site of the Village Green in 1805 in the wake of a religious revival after the Revolutionary War. The present church was erected in 1849. If the front doors are open, walk inside to admire the original tin ceiling and walls, and the spare whiteness of this church that eschews pageantry to place the emphasis on the Bible itself and the word of God. In 1849 the Dutch Reformed Church, with its principal church in Kingston, was the strongest in Ulster County, but Woodstock was the first to have a resident minister.

Early congregants spoke a mixture of Dutch and English, few knew how to read or write, and most believed in witches. Early ministers fought to ban alcohol sales, and succeeded in 1879—for a time. Yet the first Dutch immigrants weren't religious refugees like many other colonial settlers. They arrived in New Amsterdam and ventured north to make their fortunes in the New World.

The **Reformed Church of Woodstock**, as it's now named, owns the largest part of the Village Green, formerly its front yard.

The shops along the north side of the Green occupy the former **Captain Charles H. Krack House** (4 Old Forge Road), constructed as a cube-shaped hotel in the 1870's for summer boarders and visitors. There were upstairs and downstairs verandahs on two sides, plus a cupola on top. Captain Krack was both the local assemblyman in the state legislature and a New York City businessman who made his fortune by running a fancy floating bathhouse anchored in the East River. In the 1920's, the Krack House was run as The Old Woodstock Inn, with space for an art gallery. Later the verandahs were removed along with the cupola, and the current portico facing the Village Green was added.

One of the charms of the village is that so many shops are in old houses with so much history. Take **Lily's** boutique (24 Tinker Street), for example, with the old front porch and sidewalk hitching post that hasn't seen a horse in years. Floor planks of southern pine in the back room date back to the Civil War; the kerosene stove to 1906. In the early decades of the 1900's the place was both a family home and a favorite hangout known as Aunt Nellie Mower's Ice Cream Parlor, which sold both homemade and Albany ice cream, and boasted of the first telephone in town. In the 1930's it was The Knife and Fork restaurant with outdoor tables. It later became a "5 and 10" cent store and then a real estate office. The one thing it hasn't been is a post office, though you'll see old post office boxes on the wall behind the counter. They're a memento saved from the Shady post office in the 1960's. Notice the name in the upper right hand corner. Yes, **Bob Dylan** once collected mail from that box.

Formed in 1919, the **Woodstock Art Association** (28 Tinker Street) built its gallery in 1921 on the site of the A.D. Rose General Store, which had been destroyed by fire in 1911. **Birge Harrison**, a landscape artist who taught at the Byrdcliffe colony and then at the Art Students League summer school, recruited **William A. Boring**, head of the Columbia School of Architecture, to design this gallery with a colonial façade reminiscent of Woodstock's earliest buildings a century earlier. (Boring had co-designed the main building on Ellis Island.) Though the building is rather restrained, he added the oval windows for a fun flourish.

Some artists lived in town year round, but many summered here and had studios and galleries in Manhattan. The WAA gave them a gallery to show their work to each other. They sought to bridge the divide in artistic styles by granting five board seats each to the "Radical" and "Conservative" "elements." At the time some Woodstock artists eagerly followed the radical changes in European art such as Cubism that had caused a sensation at the Armory Show of 1913. These innovators soon looked to American folk art, as well, for new approaches. The conservative painters stuck to the Impressionist style that was taught in the art academies.

Among the prominent Woodstock artists who've been WAA members are **Arnold Blanch**, **Yasuo Kuniyoshi**, **Doris Lee**, **Eugene Speicher**, **George Bellows**, **Konrad Cramer**, **Leon Kroll**, **Peggy Bacon**, and the five founders, **John F. Carlson**, **Frank Swift Chase**, **Andrew Dasburg**, **Carl Eric Lindin**, and **Henry Lee McFee**. A 1938 *Life* magazine profile of the colony called the WAA the "local Louvre" and said that "Artistically Woodstock is definitely left. Its most famous color is dirty brown. For years it tried to keep out Jews."

Now renamed the **Woodstock Artists Association & Museum**, the group has assembled a permanent collection of 2,100 art works from the region that has become an invaluable record of arts colony history. A rear wing added in 1992 presents shows from this historical collection. Meanwhile, WAAM has 350 current members who display new works in group exhibitions and solo shows in the front galleries. A popular event is the Woodstock Fine Art Auction held ever Labor Day weekend. Since 2005, the **Woodstock Arts Consortium** has coordinated gallery openings on Second Saturdays. The WAAM seems to draw the liveliest crowds. One February, Nude Sushi was served from the backs of two models lying on tables while clad in several large leaves. That was an evening to warm the heart.

❈ ❈ ❈

In 1978 Barry Samuels and Ellen Shapiro leased an empty storefront to establish **The Golden Notebook** bookstore (29 Tinker Street) named after a Doris Lessing novel that was a favorite of Ellen's. From the late 1940's through the 1960's, the place had been Joe Forno's Colonial Pharmacy, a popular soda fountain shop with swivel stools at the counter and a checker tiled floor. For youngsters, this hangout was the equivalent of today's mall. (Forno was also a town judge who held court in the back of the store.)

Inspired by a *New York* magazine article about the return of independent bookstores in the wake of Barnes & Noble's troubles, Jacqueline Kellachan and Paul McMenemy bought the business in 2010 and now host frequent author events to promote new books by local and visiting writers. Among the better known authors in town are novelists **Gail Godwin, Chuck Wachtel, Jocelyn Lieu,** and **James Lasdun**; memoirists **Shalom Auslander, Abigail Thomas** and **Susan Richards**; mystery writers **Larry Beinhardt, Marshall Karp,** and **Alison Gaylin**; non-fiction authors **Peter Occhiogrosso, Clark Strand,** and **Sheila Isenberg**; poet **Ed**

Sanders; astronomer **Bob Berman**; spiritual writer **Elizabeth Lesser**; children's author **Ann Martin**, and musicians who write, such as **Steve Earle**.

❖　❖　❖

Long known as the **DeForest House** (34 Tinker Street), this 18th century building was the home of the operator of the leather tanning mill on Tannery Brook. Since then, it has been occupied by grocers, politicians, craftsmen, and then by the Jack Horner Shop before becoming, in 1945, the home of **The Woodstock Guild of Craftsmen** (now the **Woodstock Byrdcliffe Guild**), which was formed in 1938 by local artisans. By the 1950's the Guild had more than 200 members, many of whom sold their wares in the front shop, while classes were held in the basement for jewelry making, weaving, and pottery. Now the shops are leased to private businesses.

The adjacent **Kleinert/James Arts Center** (36 Tinker Street) was built in 1958 thanks to a gift from the poet Lenore G. Marshall in memory of two Woodstockers: her mother, a musician, and her aunt, Herminie Kleinert, a painter. (Board member Doug James

financed later renovations.) The gallery relies upon independent curators who present a wide range of art. Every December, there's a 5"by 7" show at which dozens of little canvases are hung anonymously and offered for $100 apiece. If you have a sharp eye or dumb luck, you might buy at this bargain price a piece by one of the town's most acclaimed artists, such as **Milton Glaser**, **Joan Synder**, **Stella Chasteen**, **Donald Elder**, or **Tricia Cline**.

In 1975 the Guild received the Byrdcliffe property upon the death of Peter Whitehead, the founder's last surviving son. By the 1980's, the **Woodstock Guild** was offering daring film festivals ("Eros and Thanatos" was one theme), publishing conferences, jazz concert series, poetry readings by, say, **Allen**

Ginsberg, musical performances by **Ed Sanders and the Fugs**, and much, much more at the Kleinert or the Byrdcliffe Theater thanks to generous New York State arts funding. Alas, that era of largesse is over. The Kleinert still hosts concerts and author events, but not on such a scale. The gift shop offers pieces by several potters who teach workshops up at Brydcliffe.

❖ ❖ ❖

Tanneries were operating on Tannery Brook by 1816, and they lasted until 1879, employing tanners and local woodsmen. The key resource was hemlock bark stripped from trees in the spring, then hauled out in winter by ox-drawn sledges. (The lore that the Catskills were once the Blue Mountains blanketed with hemlocks now lost to us forever is fanciful. The woodsmen left smaller trees that have grown into mature groves today.) The bark was ground up and leached for tannins to cure animal hides into leather for local shoe and harness makers.

❖ ❖ ❖

In the early days a millpond on Tannery Brook was the scene of witch trials-by-dunking. "If they floated, it was because their master (The Devil) was supporting them," Woodstock historian Alf Evers noted. "If they sank, they were fished out as innocent."

Since its founding, Woodstock had a tradition of belief in witches which other citizens of Ulster County mocked. Famous 19th century witches included Aunt Zantee, who cast spells on the livestock of her enemies, and Mrs. Grimm, who could take the shape of a white partridge that hunters could not shoot except with a silver bullet. Mrs. Grimm lived on Ohayo Mountain Road, on the Glenford side. Other witches lived in the Yerry Hill-Montoma area and in Mink Hollow. Some of these women gained reputations as "white" or good witches because of their abilities as healers.

Built on the site of an early grist mill followed by a saw mill, **The Old Forge** (54 Tinker Street) has changed identities many times, reflecting the village's transformations from an early tannery hamlet to an arts colony to a tourist attraction. (In 2011 the storefront joined the local "Tie Dye Wars," as shops compete for the renewed enthusiasm for the 1960's among young and old alike.) The plaque on a rock in front tells the full story of this building remodeled and preserved in 1964. In the mid-19th century The Old Forge was a blacksmith shop where wagons and carriages were kept. Horses were stabled across the street.

Once Irving Riseley's barn, the building with an open sunken porch now housing the **Center for Photography at Woodstock (59**

Tinker Street) has seen many uses. Once it was an undertaker's and an art supply store. For years, it was a soda fountain called The Nook, popular among children who came in after ice skating on Tannery Brook to warm up with hot chocolate. By the 1960's it was the Café Espresso, a Parisian-style bistro that brought Greenwich Village-like glamor upstate. Then came the Tinker Street Café, a music venue where one could sit and people watch. The photography center took over the full building in 1999 after major renovations.

In 1963 or 1964 you might have seen **Bob Dylan** here, seated at the long family table, playing chess or chatting with friends like **John Sebastian** or **Joan Baez**. A guest at his manager **Albert Grossman's** estate down the road in Bearsville, Dylan found the Café Espresso's owners to be like family and once lived upstairs for a few months, using what the called the "White Room" as his studio to compose songs for *Another Side of Bob Dylan* and *Bringing It All Back Home.* At the time he was going electric, delving into drugs, and turning surreal in his lyrics, inspired by hipster slang, the French symbolist poets such as Arthur Rimbaud, and the Beats such as **Allen Ginsberg**, who visited him in Woodstock.

A few years later, he bought his own places in town, first a house up in Byrdcliffe, then one on Ohayo Mountain Road. After a motorcycle accident on Streibel Road in July, 1966, he quit touring and had a fertile period jamming in the basement of a pink house rented in Saugerties by members of **The Band**. That house, made famous by The Band's classic 1968 album *Music from Big Pink*, is still pink, but privately owned, so don't intrude. In 1970 Dylan left Woodstock for good. Unlike other celebrities who've enjoyed semi-anonymity in town, he'd felt invaded by the disturbed pilgrims searching for him as "the Prince of Protest."

The photography center opened its gallery upstairs in 1977, founded by four lens masters tired of trying to persuade other arts organizations that photography was a worthy art form. At the time, there was a "photography liberation movement" that led to similar centers in Syracuse, Boston, San Francisco, and elsewhere. The one in Woodstock opened big with an inaugural show of work by **Walker Evans** and **Russell Lee**, who'd quit the Maverick (after losing his wife, **Doris Lee** to **Arnold Blanch**) to become a prominent Depression-era photographer. Nationally-known figures still show and teach workshops, but the center also helps regional photographers with grants and exhibitions. Since 1978, the center has held the now longest running photography benefit auction in the country, offering works by grand masters as well as hot up-and-comers

Established as a boarding house in 1926, **Twin Gables** (73 Tinker Street) is the oldest inn in town. The current owner has sought to keep the "American grandma" period style, though "country French" has appeared as rooms are refurbished.

In 1979 the town moved many of its offices from Tinker Street to a former estate on Comeau Drive. But **Town Hall** (76 Tinker Street), built in 1938, still houses town court and the police department in woefully cramped quarters. (A warning to lawbreakers: if arrested you may be cuffed to a radiator for lack of anyplace else to put you.)

The politics behind the building are revealing. In 1936 Carl Eric Lindin, an artist and Democratic leader, proposed a grander town hall that would have included a theater auditorium and an art gallery. The funding would have come in large part from President Roosevelt's Works Progress Administration. But local Republicans hated the New Deal, so they

rejected his suggestion by two to one in a town vote, and built this more modest town hall, instead. The arts colony notwithstanding, Woodstock was a rural Republican stronghold until IBM's arrival brought cosmopolitan professionals as full-time residents. By the 1980's the two parties were evenly matched. Now, the local Republican party has shrunken to a four to one disadvantage as its elderly members have died or moved to Florida. The Democrats are left to fighting among themselves. After the Democratic primaries, the losers may run as Republicans in the general election, and sometimes they win.

The previous building on the site was the Fireman's Hall, built in 1911. The hall was a community meeting room, and was rented to the Woodstock Club, which hosted the town's first motion picture showings. Costumes were made in the hall for Woodstock's Sesquicentennial in the 1930s.

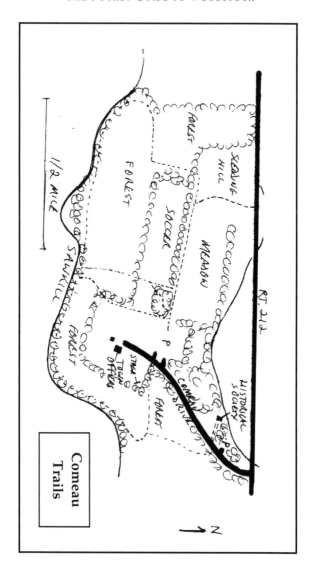

Comeau Trails

1/2 MILE

FOREST

SLEDDING HILL

FOREST

SOCCER

MEADOW

SAWKILL

FOREST

TOWN OFFICES

COMEAU DRIVE

FOREST

HISTORICAL SOCIETY

RT. 212

N

For many years the Town Hall was Woodstock's movie theater. Two features a week were shown, the first on Friday and Saturday, the second Sunday and Monday. By tradition, boys sat on the right, girls on the left.

Started in the Café Espresso in 1963, **Performing Arts of Woodstock** has staged plays here for years, engaging the public with serious dramas that may be less familiar, rather than settling for the hoary chestnuts of community theater. They prefer to be thought of as Little Theater, invoking the tradition that began with Eugene O'Neill and the Provincetown Players in the 1910's.

The **Comeau Property** is Woodstock's Central Park, offering soccer fields, dog walks, woodland trails beside the Sawkill; and an outdoor stage for **Bird-On-A-Cliff's** summer Shakespeare productions with a twist, such as *As You Like It* performed by Beatniks with bongos or *Much Ado About Nothing* dressed up as a Wild, Wild West Show.

The trails are a treat. They skirt the playing fields and loop down alongside the stream. They pass under white pines grown up in former fields and a hemlock grove beside the stream cascades over bedrock waterfalls. To help walkers across muddy stretches, a volunteer trail crew has put it a raised walkway made from sections of the Coney Island Boardwalk, which was being dismantled in favor of concrete. The longest trail loop is about a mile.

The **Town Offices** at the top of the hill occupy the former summer home of the **Edgar Eames** family of Montclair, New Jersey. Mr. Eames made his wealth at the silk trade in Manhattan. He hired architect **Frank E. Wallis**, a prominent proponent of the colonial style, to build this Dutch influenced-house in 1911, which also features elements of the Arts and Crafts style seen at Byrdcliffe. **John F. Carlson**, a family friend and arts colony figure, painted the landscape over the mantelpiece, a scene that reminds us that Woodstock was once a valley of pastures.

The Eameses didn't mingle. They might be glimpsed leaving their long driveway in a long touring car driven by a chauffeur. But their daughter, who inherited the property, did become active in local life and married

Martin Comeau, who served as the town lawyer. In 1979, after their deaths, the town bought the estate.

The **Eames House**, formerly an artist's studio for many years, is now home to the **Historical Society of Woodstock** (20 Comeau Drive), founded in 1929. It mounts exhibitions every summer and fall that bring the past to life. One summer members planted a World War II era Victory Garden in the yard. Open weekend afternoons.

❧ ❧ ❧

Here's a geology puzzle: how is the Comeau both a hill and a lake bottom? Catskills geologist **Robert Titus** has found evidence for both having been created by the advance and retreat of Ice Age glaciers. Eroded Sawkill stream banks at the western end reveal telltale layers of lake sediment. Those that are thicker and sandier alternate with those that are thinner and siltier, a pattern created by lake ice melting and forming above. During summer, sand blew into the open water. In winter silt drifted down from the ice. Glacial Lake Woodstock would have been dammed by a towering glacier wall still filling the valley to the east. The flat terrain from the village to Bearsville was a lake bottom 280 feet deep.

The hill formed later during the last glacial advance up the Sawkill Valley. As the ice pushed around uplifted bedrock at this point, it deposited soil on the far side to create a drumlin, a smooth, spoon-shaped hill. As you look around at the surrounding hills try to find the low spot where Glacial Lake Woodstock would have drained to the west. It turns out to be a notch at the top of Wittenberg Road. To look out across the Woodstock valley from that notch today is to realize that this ancient lake must have been an Ice Age version of the Ashoken Reservoir, smaller, perhaps, but also deeper.

The unusually large skylight of the **Christian Science Church** (89 Tinker Street) reveals its origins as the studio built in 1912 for the Summer School of the Art Students League of New York City. The school opened in 1906 with about 25 students who met in a barn, but grew to 200 young people by the 1910's who brought vitality—and money— to an aging community. (They also brought nude models who posed by the streams, a ravishing sight not soon forgotten by some locals.) The League held classes in Woodstock until 1922, then returned in 1947 to the buildings on Route 212 now used by the Woodstock School of Art.

The building became a church in 1923. One longtime local says that it has hardly changed, save for the loss of a triple-seater outhouse in back. He admits that as kids "We tipped it over every Halloween."

At the **Woodstock Library** (5 Library Lane), the smaller section to the west is the oldest part, built in 1812. (Note the 18 cut-out stars for each state in the Union at that time.) The home of a doctor, Larry Gilbert Hall, this portion once stood closer to Tinker Street.

The library was founded in a converted barn elsewhere on Tinker Street in 1912 as part of the Woodstock Club, which leased this building in 1926. Today the library is far more active than you'd expect for a town of this size and has a particularly notable art book collection, as well as interesting art on the walls. On many Saturdays during the summer the Friends of the Library, incorporated in 1990, opens the book barn in back for one of the best used book sales in the region.

In keeping with the library's educational tradition, the trees on the lawn wear identification tags. After heavy rains, the large pool that lingers on the lawn is known as Lake Woodstock, one of the quirks of this beloved institution. Held on the final Saturday in July of every year since 1931, the Woodstock Library Fair is the town's largest and oldest community celebration. Book sales, children's activities, food, and music attract over 5,000 people annually. Local politicians running for office are guaranteed to meet and greet the public.   Woodstock has long been an eclectic community of people with unusual careers and amateur scholarly pursuits. Since 1986, the Woodstock Library

Forum has given them the chance to address the public on Saturdays at 5 pm.. One week the subject might be the Parthenon's architecture, the next Medicare reform. It's the mid-Hudson's longest running cultural and public affairs forum.

There are a dozen Woodstocks in the country, most of them villages smaller than ours, which was the third after earlier settlements in New Hampshire and Connecticut. The English village of Woodstock north of Oxford derived its name from the Saxon "wudestoc" for clearing in the forest. Today, that town is best known for Blenheim Palace, birthplace of Winston Churchill. The library has a cornerstone that was a gift from this original Woodstock. But it's not clear that we took our name from England. Some think

that our Woodstock is an Anglicization of the Indian name for this area "Waghkonk."

Across the street is a two story house built in 1850 by Dr. Stephen Heath, who was a Woodstock Town Supervisor. Now the **Heath House** (95 Tinker Street) is the home of the **Gilded Carriage**, a fine kitchen and tableware store since 1959, which has expanded while retaining its historic appearance.

In the early 1900's a Mrs. Cooper ran a boarding house here for summer students from the Art Students League. For 25 cents, a student could enjoy not only a large lunch, but the use of Mrs. Cooper's verandah, parlor, and lawn for social events. Students played instruments, danced, sang, and courted—and held wrestling matches. As a young man, artist Ned Chase (grandfather of comedian Chevy Chase) won a wrestling match with Mr. Lasher from the funeral home across the street, but three months later Mr. Lasher bested him. Mrs. Cooper's husband was a butcher who had lopped off his finger while cutting sausage. He used to tell the students that it still itched, and he'd scratch the phantom finger with his butcher knife.

In front of the Heath House stands a metal sculpture of a boar. People who have traveled to Florence, Italy may recognize it as a copy of Il Porcellino, which stands in the Mercato Nuovo. Legend says that if you rub his snout you will return.

❖ ❖ ❖

In the late 19th Century there was talk of bringing the railroad to town. That never happened, but businessman Victor Basil hauled one of the Ulster & Delaware's former railroad stations from Hurley in 1970, and set it across Tinker Street from **Lasher's Funeral Home** (100 Tinker Street)—creating a symbolic entrance to town across from a real exit. Basil opened a barber shop in back and a beauty parlor up front. He added a side porch and a rooftop cupola that gave the station the swagger found in a John Wayne western. Over a century ago this building served Browns Station, a hamlet flooded by the Ashokan Reservoir.

❖ ❖ ❖

Housed in a former Methodist church built in 1832, the **Tinker Street Cinema** (132 Tinker Street) hasn't changed much since opening in 1967, or since **Jimi Hendrix** tried out his version of the "Star Spangled Banner" at a jam the weekend before he played the 1969 testival. The following summer, the cinema hosted the world premiere of the film documentary, *Woodstock*, an early case of the town taking credit for the concert that didn't happen here. The theater owner feared that he'd be overrun by thousands of music fans, but only had to turn away 32.

In November, 1977 Cyrus and Nancy Adler bought the business. He'd been a New York City lawyer. She was a young mother. That winter brought nothing but snow and ice. Filmgoers were few and far between. The Adlers feared they'd made a big mistake. On June 1st, they opened Woody Allen's *Manhattan* and discovered the joy of having a hit. Woody Allen's films have continued to "break the bank" ever since then, a reminder that Woodstock can seem like the Upper Upper West Side or Greenwich Village North, depending on your city loyalties.

Since 2010, Upstate Films of Rhinebeck has run the theater.

❖ ❖ ❖ ❖ ❖ ❖ ❖ ❖ ❖ ❖ ❖ ❖ ❖ ❖ ❖ ❖ ❖

OTHER HOUSES OF WORSHIP

❖ ❖ ❖ ❖ ❖ ❖ ❖ ❖ ❖ ❖ ❖ ❖ ❖ ❖ ❖ ❖ ❖

The Methodists were the third congregation to form in Woodstock, starting at a private home in Bearsville in 1828 before building their Tinker Street church in 1832, followed by five more churches in the area. Modern times brought consolidation. After two local congregations merged into one at the Tinker Street church, they sought more room and better parking. The modern, California-style **Overlook United Methodist Church** was built out of bluestone and redwood down the road at 233 Tinker Street and opened in 1967.

After assembling for several years in a converted corncrib guest house heated by a pot-bellied stove, the Episcopalians built their dramatic, A-framed **Saint Gregory's Church** (2578 Route 212) in 1957. The peaked roof was meant to reflect the mountains in the distance, which were more visible before the background trees grew to maturity. Artist

Eduardo Chavez contributed the altar cross, a boldly abstract metal sculpture. Saint Gregory is the patron saint of the arts.

In 1986 an ad in the *Woodstock Times* invited Jews to a bagel brunch to plan celebrations for the High Holy Days. A surprising number showed up, causing some to say to others, "I didn't know you were Jewish!" As word spread, plans for the ceremony had to be expanded until an outdoor tent was rented for more than 250 attendees. A few years later, the Reformist **Kehillat Lev Shalem— Woodstock Jewish Congregation** recruited **Rabbi Jonathan Kligler** from a seminary in Philadelphia. A popular figure, he's now well known for picking up his guitar and singing as part of his services. After meeting for years in a rental property, the congregation moved to its large new synagogue at 1682 Glasco Turnpike in 2006.

Rock City Road

(Walking north from the Village Green)

At the yellow **Chamber of Commerce & Arts** information booth (10 Rock City Road), you'll find maps and brochures, and up-to-the-minute information on events. For the camera happy, sculptor Ze'ev Willy Neumann has installed a big red picture frame in front of a purple bench where you may have your photo snapped for "15 Minutes of Frame."

From the booth lawn, you see to the north majestic Overlook Mountain, which had bluestone quarries along its flanks in the 19th century. The largest of them, California Quarry, was worked by immigrants settled in the Irish village in Lewis Hollow.

Most of the bluestone was used for common sidewalks, but competition arose among Gilded Age millionaires for the biggest sidewalk stones to place in front of their Manhattan mansions. Every so often, a prized monstrous-sized slab emerged from a Woodstock quarry to be loaded onto a wagon, which caused the wheels to sink several inches in the dirt, and then be hauled through the village as everyone wondered if the bridges would hold. Sometimes they didn't. Supposedly, one 20-ton stone pulled by 17 horses broke every bridge from Woodstock to its Hudson River loading dock.

The name, Rock City Road, originated in the old-timers' saying, "If we had as many people as rocks, we'd have a city."

The Chamber of Commerce & Arts booth sits on the site of a crime. Here stood a noble Victorian building, the mansard-roofed Brinkerhof-Longyear House, built in 1870. The mansard roof emulated that of the Overlook Mountain House which opened in 1871; William Brinkerhof was a major investor. That grand hotel burned on April Fool's Day, 1875 to be replaced by a second Overlook Mountain House, which later burned, and almost a third, the ruins of which still stand half-a-mile from the summit. In 1974, the bank's owners promised to consider preserving the Brinkerhof-Longyear House, but instead razed it in the middle of the night, an act of vandalism that should serve as a warning to citizens hoping to preserve their architectural heritage. (The Captain Krack

House across the street offers some idea of what was lost.)

The Woodstock Film Festival has spawned the Hudson Valley Film Commission to help movies get made in our midst. Together, they share offices in the blue building (13 Rock City Road) owned for decades by Adolph Heckeroth, the town plumber. After World War II, a young Marine veteran named Lee Marvin moved here and worked for Heckeroth. Among his jobs, he was a "honey dipper" who emptied septic systems. While working on plumbing at the Woodstock Playhouse, he was invited to fill in for a sick actor. By 1950 he'd performed Off Broadway and gone to Hollywood. Upon moving into this building, the film festival staff found, perhaps as a ghostly welcome, Lee Marvin's handwriting scribbled on a rusty Kelvinator refrigerator.

Other Hollywood celebrities have graced Woodstock, such as **Uma Thurman**, whose father, **Robert Thurman**, a Buddhist scholar at Columbia University, has owned a house here for years. But nobody has left as many colorful stories as Lee Marvin. In 1970 he returned to care for his ailing father and married an old sweetheart. They later moved to Arizona.

Now brown, the former barn at 15 Rock City Road was once the **S.S. Sea Horse**, a popular watering hole for locals and artists alike from the late 1940's into the early 1960's. Patrons enjoyed many a memorable night, especially the finalé. Dick Stillwater, the owner, bent down behind the bar for a bottle and didn't bend up. His corpse was laid under a sheet on the Ping-Pong table, while everyone enjoyed free rounds in his honor. Not for two hours did anyone think to call the authorities. When a state trooper finally arrived in the doorway, he gave a stern look and reprimanded the room. "Two hours ago?" he said. "Do you know what that means? It means you've all got a two-hour head start! Somebody pour me a drink!"

In the late 1960's the place flourished anew as a music venue called the **Elephant**. But the owner, who'd been convicted of drug charges, wasn't allowed a liquor license, so the Elephant was converted into a boutique that later closed.

❖ ❖ ❖

Family of Woodstock (16 Rock City Road) began with a phone number. After the 1969 festival, the two constables in town felt besieged by hippies camping on lawns, runaways suffering bad acid trips, and weirdos looking for Bob Dylan. At a community meeting held to find a better answer than busting everybody, Gail Varsi told the police to give these troubled youngsters her home number—679-2485—on Library Lane. (Perhaps she empathized because her older sister, Diane Varsi, after being touted as "Hollywood's Female Brando" for her supporting role in *Peyton Place* in 1957, had later suffered a breakdown.) Whenever Gail Varsi went out, she had a volunteer sit by her phone. Thus began the 24-hour hot line still answered by volunteers today, the second oldest such hot line in the country. Granted, there are now 10 more phone lines and volunteers have received 35 hours of training, but the motto remains the same: "Any problem under the sun."

Months after the hot line started, volunteers formed a group called the Soft Landing Machine to go out and meet with people suffering bad trips. Out of these efforts grew Family of Woodstock, a social services organization which has its headquarters in Kingston, additional offices in Ellenville and New Paltz, and some 160 employees and just as many volunteers. It addresses domestic abuse, homelessness, and other problems.

This two story house was given to Family in 1974 and consecrated by supporters who gathered in a circle around the building. Inside is a " Free Store" of clothes, "Free Bread" on a rack, a small waiting area, and a counter manned by volunteers. For a time, the group also ran a homeless shelter in town.

All of this doesn't mean you won't see characters on the Village Green who look like graying hippies still on the loose after the 1969 festival. Street people have been a part of Woodstock ever since then. Some have been fascinating figures. Silent Mark Rogosin, for instance, had been a world-traveling patent attorney with a Fifth Avenue apartment until he left posh respectability for the streets, where, if he liked you, he'd hand you the gift of a small rock he'd painted with a Tibetan Buddhist symbol.

❧ ❧ ❧

The **Colony Café** (22 Rock City Road) was built in 1929 by Gabriel Newgold as a hotel in an un-Woodstock Moorish style of brick and stucco. It was originally intended to be an overnight lodge for guests on their way up to the Overlook Mountain House for longer stays. But the Mountain House, then being rebuilt after a fire, never re-opened, and the Colony went on to a checkered existence, flourishing at times as a hotel, dance hall, and arts exhibition space. In its early days a popular cafeteria and bakery operated in the basement. But it has stood fallow for long periods, and now struggles with winter heating bills, while presenting local musicians. The interior ballroom with a wooden balcony, a long wooden bar, and a large stone fireplace offers the most romantic performance space in town.

The **Lotus Galley** (33 Rock City Road) is the site of more memorable nights. It was **Deanie's Brass Rail Tavern** in the 1940's. Then **Buckman's**, **Shannon's**, and the **Village Jug** in the 1960's and 1970's, home of Wednesday Peanut Night and Sunday morning Bloody Mary softball league. And, finally, **Rosa's Cantina**, where in 1975 "Magic Markie" (Mark Gondleman), who owned the town's first head shop, aimed for and surely achieved a Guinness world record by DJing for 33 1/3 straight days while taking 20 minute naps. "I had a physician in attendance who certified I was drug-free throughout," he told a reporter. "I feel fine, though I have a bit of a throat condition."

In the **Woodstock Cemetery** the graves of Woodstock's founding families are located on a ridge up the drive to the right when you enter the grounds. See if you can find the grave of Catherine Van De Bogart, aged 18, buried with her infant in 1821, the victim of her husband John's cruelty. An elm tree once towered over the gravestone, a reminder of one of Woodstock's great legends. John Van De Bogart, a middle-aged husband, was acutely jealousy of his beautiful wife. Arriving home one evening for supper only to find his house empty, he suspected the worst and cut a stick from an elm tree. Upon her return (she'd been visiting a sick neighbor), he beat her so savagely that she died the next day while giving birth. She'd asked to be buried with the stick so that it might take root in her heart and grow as a reminder to her husband that her love had been true. For early art students, this tale added to the romantic aura of Woodstock.

The Woodstock Memorial Day Parade, one of the town's cherished traditions, finishes at the cemetery after marching through the village. Everyone joins in, from volunteer firemen riding their trucks to Little Leaguers tossing out candies from their parade floats. Veterans for Peace stand by silently holding protest signs. By the cemetery flagpole at the end, rifles are aimed, volleys are fired, and little boys scramble for spent shells. The flag is raised. Taps is played, sad and haunting. A young girl sings the "Star Spangled Banner."

❖ ❖ ❖

Across the road, hidden beyond the parking lot, is the **Artists' Cemetery**, where generations of Woodstock artists lie, separated from ordinary citizens. Follow Mountainview Avenue and walk up through the graveyard. In 1934 the Kingsbury family buried their son near the top of the hill after he'd been killed in a car accident soon after his prep school graduation. Dr. John Kingsbury was a prominent public health advocate for the poor who alienated some with his sympathies for Russia, but charmed others with his all-night star parties to observe the Perseid meteor showers. He also collected wild mushrooms and held dinner parties at which the lights were briefly turned off so that his guests could see the fungi bioluminenscing on their plates. The family hadn't intended for the cemetery to be for artists, but it has filled with arts colony figures. Down in a hollow is a memorial to Byrd-cliffe Colony founders **Jane and Ralph**

Radcliffe Whitehead—a Della Robbia-style Virgin and Child brought from Italy.

In this necropolis you'll also find markers for **Bolton Brown** and **Hervey White**, Byrdcliffe's other founders. See who else you recognize among the famous and semi-famous—like the painter **Milton Avery** or the composer **Robert Starer**. It's not morbid to visit grave sites, rather a way of remembering the brevity of our time here.

In the 1920's the Colony Café was a controversial building seen as garish and out-of-place in a village that favored the Greek Revival style. You can't miss today's architectural controversy across the street, a private residence dubbed **Logstock** at 39 Rock City Road. Montana has invaded the Catskills.

The brown shingle structure built in 1922 as the St. Joan D'Arc Catholic Church is now the **Mescal Hornbeck Community Center** (56 Rock City Road) named after a beloved activist who died in 2011 at age 99. Her personality? "Cantankerous," said an old friend approvingly. Among her crusades was saving this building from demolition after the Catholics moved to **St. John's Roman Catholic Church** in West Hurley. Like most public buildings in town, the Community Center could use refurbishing, but it's kept busy with meetings, senior rec programs (yoga, Tai-Chi/Qi Gong, etc.), and Sunday afternoon drumming.

Since 1975 Family has sponsored an annual Thanksgiving dinner at the center that has become a major community event. Upwards of 500 people attend this feast of donated foods that range from a restaurant's *nouvelle cuisine* to Mom's yam pie. A Congressman might sit next to a homeless woman. It's a time to put aside differences and celebrate.

The **Andy Lee Memorial Field** was farmland until it was purchased in the 1920's by the Woodstock Athletic Club, whose members included **Ralph Whitehead**, **John F. Carlson**, and painter **George Bellows**, an avid baseball player. Now it's a town park with ball fields, a basketball court, and a swimming pool for children's summer day camp. (Seventeen year old Andy Lee died in a winter hunting accident in 1956, when his companion slipped on the ice and shot him in the throat. Lee had recently been voted the most popular student at Kingston High School.) Beyond the ball fields is a community garden fenced against the deer.

❖ ❖ ❖ ❖ ❖ ❖ ❖ ❖ ❖ ❖ ❖ ❖ ❖ ❖ ❖ ❖ ❖

ANOTHER TOWN PARK

❖ ❖ ❖ ❖ ❖ ❖ ❖ ❖ ❖ ❖ ❖ ❖ ❖ ❖ ❖ ❖ ❖

For generations, little leaguers played baseball at Andy Lee field. In the 1980's the game moved across across town to the diamond at **Rick Volz Field** (34 Dixon Avenue) which the Volz family from the neighborhood had been voluntarily grooming for sandlot games. Now the field boasts an impressive little league stadium. Beyond the field in the woods known as Mallory Grove, the **Woodstock Dog Park** opened in 2011 to let dogs run unleashed among the trees within two large fenced areas.

❖ ❖ ❖ ❖ ❖ ❖ ❖ ❖ ❖ ❖ ❖ ❖ ❖ ❖ ❖ ❖ ❖

Built in 1898 as a private mansion used by a succession of farm families, the **Wild Rose Inn** (66 Rock City Road) opened in 1998 in what had become an apartment house. The new owner painted the maroon trim to bring out the fun in the Victorian style.

An early Woodstock leader, John Wigram, had built his house at this site in 1806. He served as supervisor, brought the post office to town, collected rent from the tenant farmers on behalf of the Livingstons, worked as a land surveyor, and also farmed using slaves, who stayed after being freed by law in 1827. One former slave was Tim Wigram, who had a wooden leg supposedly made from a bedpost. At a roadside stand he sold sarsaparilla root beer, chewing gum, and molasses candy. He planted a cottonwood, which until the 1950's was the biggest tree in town.

❖ ❖ ❖

At the corner with Lower Byrdcliffe Road, look left into **Parnassus Square**. This barn, while not truly Dutch, is a fine example of the many barns which once stood in a more rural Woodstock. In later years it housed art galleries like the Artists Cooperative in the mid-1970's and then the Night Gallery.

In the 1940's **George Ault**, a reclusive painter, did a series of night scenes at this intersection, then called **Russell's Corners**, that showed little more than red and white barns lit by a solitary street lamp against the black night. Now considered masterpieces, these paintings were featured in a Smithsonian exhibit in 2011. From this most ordinary of settings, he was able to conjure the somber mood of our nation during World War II.

Not far away on what is now **Bellows Lane** lived **George Bellows** with his family in the 1920's, when he was one of the highest paid artists in America. His good friend and neighbor, **Eugene Speicher**, was considered the country's finest portraitist. Another neighbor and close friend, the painter **Charles Rosen**, had moved from Pennsylvania, where he'd been a master of the established Impressionist style, to Woodstock, where he'd ventured in the radical new direction towards Cubism.

Today, four artists from the hundreds who came to Woodstock stand out in 20th Century American art history: **George Bellows**, **Yasuo Kuniyoshi**, **Milton Avery**, and

Philip Guston. What happened to the others, such as Speicher, now almost famous for having fallen so far into obscurity?

Tastes change. Today at the Metropolitan Museum of Art, the Catskills are the domain of the Hudson River School who painted the region from the 1820's onwards. There's scant trace of the Woodstock colony. Yet in the 1920's, the heyday of Bellows, Speicher, and Rosen, those Hudson River School paintings were held in such low repute that they would have been found in antique shops, not sullying gallery walls or museums.

At the **Four Corners**, Rock City Road crosses Glasco Turnpike to become Meads Mountain Road. On the right stands the house of seascape artist **Henry Mattson**, marked by a plaque. Early students at the art colony lived in barns, sheds, and hay lofts around the Four Corners. Calling themselves the "Barnacles," these students often gathered in a house on the northeast corner, where **Rosie Magee** kept her boarding house; her kitchen became a center of Woodstock artistic life.

For years the area was known as **Rock**

City. The arts colony was divided between traditionalists and those eager to try the newest approaches from Europe. In the 1910's the Woodstock experimenters became known as the Rock City Rebels. One day, feeling Dadaist, they declared, "Art is dead. Let us bury him." They dug a grave in front of a studio, threw in their canvases, and marked the spot with an old tombstone.

Then, no doubt, they went right back to painting.

❖ ❖ ❖

Mill Hill Road

(Walking east from the Village Green)

The white brick pediment of the **1933 Longyear Building** at the corner of Rock City and Mill Hill Roads stands over a row of shops (1-7 Mill Hill Road). **Stanley Longyear**, during the early years of the arts colony, ran the horse drawn stage coach that brought people into town from the train station in West Hurley. Prior to this building, a series of inns stood on this site dating back to the 1790's. In the earliest days these inns served travelers, but after the Civil War they housed summer boarders, city people who came to escape the heat of sweltering apartments and the stink of urban streets. Grandest of all was the **Woodstock Valley Hotel**

built in 1869 (and later called the **Irvington**) that stood three stories tall and had long double piazzas on which walking competitions were held in the 1890's, an era when pedestrianism was publicity-grabbing entertainment. That structure burned in 1930.

From World War II into the late 1970's the **Rudolph Gallery**, now Bread Alone (22 Mill Hill Road), showed many colony artists, including **Milton Avery**. Rudolph and Lillian Fiolic fell into the business by chance. In 1939, intending to move to France, they sold their antique furnishings at roadside and soon found themselves selling their friends' paintings as well. With the advent of World War II, their plans for France came to naught, so they became art dealers instead.

On Wednesday evenings from June through October, **Maple Lane** hosts the **Woodstock Farm Festival,** a farmers' market begun in 2008 that also serves as a town picnic with hot food vendors, live entertainment, and outdoor tables, where friends catch up with friends. Sustainability enthusiasts hope that the future will bring small farms back to Woodstock to sell their produce at this market.

Down Maple Lane is **Mower's Field**, where a **flea market** reminiscent of old Woodstock is held on summer weekends—and now on Wednesdays during the farmers' market. Visiting the flea market is like taking a step back in history, where everyone's attic is on display. In fact, this market traces its lineage back to the first fair held on the Village Green in 1918 as a fundraiser for the Red Cross during World War I. (Another Red Cross fundraiser, a chamber concert at the Fireman's Hall in 1914, led to the founding of the Maverick concert series.) Over the decades these outdoor markets moved about town until landing here in 1974. Three years later **John Mower**, the property owner, began managing the flea market himself.

The Mowers had come to Woodstock in the late 1860's to farm and work in the quarries on Overlook. In 1907 a family member bought a creamery on this lot that he converted into a house that would be home to three generations. By 1970, though, John Mower, then 22, and other family members lived elsewhere in the area. Vagrants who'd invaded Woodstock after the 1969 festival broke into this empty house and trashed it so badly that John let the local fire company burn it down for a fire drill. Yet sad endings can lead to happy new chapters in life. At the time, John had a job servicing cigarette vending machines. Now he enjoys spending his weekends trading stories with visitors from near and far. He has convinced a few—well, almost—that the 1969 festival took place right on his flea market lawn.

Built in 1895 **Christ's Lutheran Church** (26 Mill Hill Road) has the plain white exterior common to the village, but indoors has an unusual sanctuary made of varnished wainscoting right out of a Victorian era parlor. The 1885 Hook & Hastings organ appeals to musicians. **Garth Hudson**, The Band's keyboardist, sent students to play on it. In the 1940's **Paul Wesley Arndt** painted four large scenes from Christ's life for the sanctuary. In the Sermon on the Mount painting Christ addresses a crowd which includes the faces of Woodstockers at the time, or so the story goes. The Lutherans had established their first church near the bottom of Mill Hill Road in 1806. Longstanding Hudson Valley residents, they'd migrated from a church in Saugerties that was already 100 years old.

In 1992 **Tom Fletcher** decided that he'd had enough of being a traveling textbook salesman and opened the **Fletcher Gallery** (40 Mill Hill Road), instead. Not that he had any background as an art dealer, but he had the good fortune to befriend many of the Woodstock artists near the end of their lives. He specializes in paintings by people who were here between 1900 and 1950.

❖ ❖ ❖ ❖ ❖ ❖ ❖ ❖ ❖ ❖ ❖ ❖ ❖ ❖ ❖ ❖ ❖

GALLERY HOPPING

❖ ❖ ❖ ❖ ❖ ❖ ❖ ❖ ❖ ❖ ❖ ❖ ❖ ❖ ❖ ❖ ❖

The premier spot in Woodstock for contemporary art is the **Elena Zang Gallery** four miles west of town on Route 212 in Shady (3671 Route 212). She arrived in Woodstock in 1961 as a teenager and still glows with the memories of seeing her first art gallery, hearing her first poetry reading, and hanging out at the Café Espresso during high school amid the likes of **Bob Dylan**, **Joan Baez**, and **Tim Hardin**. In 1968 she found her own calling as a potter. For a decade she was a hippie homesteader out in Big Indian. In 1989 she and her partner, **Alan Hoffman**, also a potter, bought their property to build studios for themselves in the back barn. A year later, in addition to selling their pottery, they began showing work by artist friends, starting with the acclaimed **Mary Frank** and continuing with **Judy Pfaff**, **Joan Snyder**, **Stella Chasteen**, **Donald Elder**, **Martin Puryear**, **Melinda Stickney-Gibson** and others from the area. The grounds offer an enchanting stroll by gardens, a stream, and some 35 sculptures. There's a bronze figure by Mary Frank lying on the grass that will slip into your mythic imagination and stay.

Farther out in Willow, the **James Cox Gallery** (4666 Route 212) handles both current art and the estates of Woodstock arts colony figures. Back in town next to the Tinker Street Cinema the **VARGA Gallery** (130 Tinker Street) has the raw and funky spirit of the 1980's East Village scene with its emphasis on visionary and outsider art. You might meet **Christina Varga** herself kneeling on the floor to apply varnish to the lower corner of one of her paintings. She believes in crowding the walls of this former Methodist Church parsonage with wild and vibrant art.

❖ ❖ ❖ ❖ ❖ ❖ ❖ ❖ ❖ ❖ ❖ ❖ ❖ ❖ ❖ ❖ ❖ ❖

Not Fade Away (42 Mill Hill Road), the corner building with an outdoor deck and an indoor selection of bongs and tee-shirts, was once the **Joyous Lake**, one of the great small rock clubs in the country. Begun as a juice bar and health food eatery in 1971 by **Ron Merians**, a burly podiatrist-turned-fashion photographer, and his stunning wife, **Valma**, a former model, the place tapped into the music scene, showcasing famous performers from the area as well as bands in town to record. For locals, you had **Van Morrison**, **Paul Butterfield**, **Maria Muldaur**, and **John Sebastian**. For visitors, **Bonnie Raitt**, the **Pointer Sisters**, **Taj Mahal**, **Richie Havens, Gil Scott Heron,** the **Rolling Stones,** and many others. Great jazz as well: **Charles Mingus, Dave Holland**.

The place was a beloved madhouse. Not only did musicians play here, they held court at the bar and sometimes accepted coke lines. The waitresses wore tiny shorts and bandannas tied on as halters. People danced on the tables. Crowds jammed the sidewalks. For Baby Boomers now reflecting on their party-happy youth, those were the glory years when Woodstock was a live music town. In the 1960's and 1970's there were upwards of a dozen bars and cafés where you could find a night to remember—or forget. The Café Espresso, Rose's Cantina, the legendary Sled Hill Café on a back street. Rick Danko of The Band seemed to be everywhere.

What happened? Any veteran of those late nights will tell you that Woodstock is now dead after dark.

"The DWI laws killed live music in this town," says **Jeremy Wilber**, the town supervisor who served a youthful apprenticeship as a bartender at the Sled Hill Café. "The days of 'Thank God I've got a car because I'm too drunk to walk,' are long past." On the positive side, the fatal car crashes on Route 28 and Glasco Turnpike have declined. One night Wilber lost his car in a bar bet to a friend who then sold it to someone else who was killed in that very car by a drunk driver.

And those young ladies who danced on the Joyous Lake tables? They're now esteemed members of the **Woodstock Tennis Club.**

❖ ❖ ❖

Turning onto Elwyn Lane at the bottom of the hill, you'll see at the first bend the 1799 **Stone House** erected by Jonathan Hasbrouck, Ulster County's first judge and Wood-

stock's wealthiest inhabitant, who built this house on a 500-acre tract using bluestone quarried nearby. The construction combined Dutch stone work with the New England style for windows and doors. Compared to earlier communities in the region, Woodstock has relatively few stone houses because the preference was for "Yankee houses" made of wood.

Before the **Bradley Meadows Shopping Center** was built in 1966, the spot was a meadow favored by painters for having the best mountain view in town. Inside **Bank of America** (81 Mill Hill Road) you'll find a mural-sized landscape by Paul Wesley Arndt that depicts Woodstock as a pastoral pre-automobile paradise. Even the deer buck by the edge of an overgrown field has antlers to stir a hunter's fantasies.

By the 1920's the arts colony was in full bloom. A visiting magazine writer noted three art schools, two string quartets, two theaters, four tearooms, an art gallery, and "the long village street crowded with students in vivid garb." Actors had followed the earlier arrival of painters and crafts people. The open-air Maverick Theater debuted on July 4, 1924 with a production starring **Edward G. Robinson** and **Helen Hayes** as the ingénue. (Decades later, she recalled that she had to lie "dead" on stage through the last act while mosquitoes settled in for "banqueting.") **Paul Robeson** and **Ruth St. Denis** also appeared during the four years the theater was active. The Byrdcliffe Theater countered with the Phoenix Players.

For generations, the property by the intersection of Route 375 and Route 212 had been the Riseley family farm, one of the oldest in town. (In 1762 Robert Livingston, Woodstock's landlord, had built a mill here by the Sawkill.) In 1929 the **Woodstock Playhouse** opened in the former Riseley barn with Eugene O'Neill's "Emperor Jones," starring Charles Gilpin. Broadway theater people came to Woodstock to witness what locals called "The Battle of the Theaters" because there was so much thespian activity.

The converted barn burned in 1931. In 1938 a new **Woodstock Playhouse** went up, a striking structure with a pair of titled, arched roofs like a barn gone ulta-modern. In the ensuing decades summer stock theater became a big part of local life. In *Images of America: Woodstock*, Janine Fallon-Mower recalls "theatergoers dressed in their white elegance, pearls, fur stoles, and summer suits." Local boys got jobs parking cars. Deanie's restaurant and Café Espresso filled up at 10 PM with the after-theater crowd. Hundreds of rising young actors and actresses performed at what was one of the few equity theaters outside of New York City. Then the theater fell into long decline until arson claimed the building in 1988.

In 1991 a non-profit Woodstock Arts Board set about reviving the summer stock tradition. But good intentions can take time. In 1995 they built a band shell. In 2000 local archictect **Lester Walker** designed the rounded front entryway for the new **Woodstock Playhouse** (103 Mill Hill Road) reminiscent of the previous one. Gradually the structure expanded, but saw little use until foreclosure threatened. In 2010 the Pan American Dance Foundation, another non-profit, bought the place and transformed what had been an open-air theater with steel bleachers into a comfortable indoor space with tight but humane seating—and no mosquitoes. Their first summer stock season in 2011 augered well for more to come.

In 1929, the same year the first Playhouse opened, the **Woodstock Country Club** (114

Mill Hill Road) built a nine-hole course in what had been the Riseley's cow pasture. Early members were local business leaders and colony artists, including a Pulitzer-prize winning cartoonist who used the pen name Rube Goldberg. (Some of us think that golf itself is a Rube Goldberg invention.) Over the years the club has endured droughts,

financial pinches, and stream erosion along the Sawkill, but it continues to flourish as the **Woodstock Golf Club**, renamed in 1980. The Woodstock Open, started in 1932, is one of the oldest tournaments in the region. (We wish we could have seen the turtle races held on the 9th green in the 1930's as part of the Fourth of July festivities. Starting at the putting hole, the first turtle to crawl to the edge of the green won.) In 1968 the club placed a scenic easement on the property, protecting this lovely vista forever.

❉ ❉ ❉

The large yellow farmhouse turned restaurant (109 Mill Hill Road) was in the 19th
and early 20th centuries a summer boarding house run by Aaron Riseley, a Civil War
veteran. New Yorkers arrived by stage coach
after taking the train to West Hurley. Rustic
Woodstock appealed to these city sophis-
ticates. On occasion they posed for group
guest house pictures dressed up for fun as
country bumpkins in overalls and straw hats.

For years into the 1980's, the building
housed **Deanie's** restaurant, Woodstock's
favorite watering hole. It featured mediocre
but reliable food and an atmosphere unpre-
tentiously comfortable. Flo played the piano,
a painting of a satyr and nude hung over
the bar, and everybody who was anybody
showed up sooner or later. One night Michael
Perkins opened the front door to encounter
a familiar-looking inebriate coming at him.
He thought, "This must be an hallucination.
He looks like Liberty Valance." It was. **Lee
Marvin**, who played the title character in the
classic John Ford film, was a Woodstock native. There he was, as big in life as on screen.
It turned out that he'd offered to buy a round

at the bar, then pulled out a $1,000 dollar bill. Since Deanie's couldn't change it, he smiled, and walked.

Cucina, the present restaurant, has better food but fewer surprises.

❖   ❖   ❖

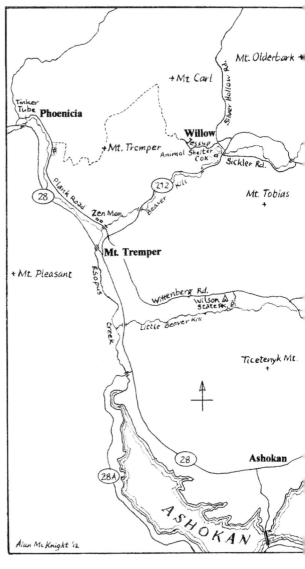

Alan McKnight '12

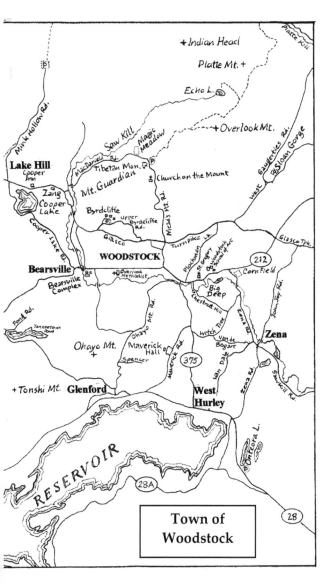

Town of
Woodstock

❖ ❖ ❖ ❖ ❖ ❖ ❖ ❖

An Arts Colony Excursion

❖ ❖ ❖ ❖ ❖ ❖ ❖ ❖

Byrdcliffe
Upper Byrdcliffe Road

In 1902 **Ralph Radcliffe Whitehead**, a wealthy, well-traveled Englishman, who'd developed Utopian ideals while studying at Oxford, sought to mend a terrible rift with his wife, **Jane Byrd McCall Whitehead**, the daughter of a former Philadelphia mayor, after she learned of his affair with another woman. At the time, they lived in an Italianate villa in Santa Barbara, California. Since their courtship a dozen years earlier, they'd shared the dream of establishing an Arts and Crafts colony of the type pioneered by

John Ruskin, Whitehead's teacher at Oxford in England in 1870. As an alternative to dehumanizing industrialization, they'd create a modern version of a Medieval guild that would restore dignity and independence to workers. To make a fresh start, they decided to move east. They hired **Bolton Brown** away from his art professorship at Stanford University to scout the Catskills.

After roaming the mountains for three weeks, finding his way "over summits so wild it seemed no man or animal could ever have been there," a terrain far worse than the California Sierra for "sheer  savage impenetrability and utter laboriousness," Brown reached the saddle on Overlook Mountain, where the KTD monastery now stands, and "like Balboa from his 'peak in Darien,' first saw my South Sea," the "extraordinarily beautiful" Woodstock Valley as "wide and almost as blue as the sea" with "the silver Hudson losing itself in the remote haze."

Within a year Whitehead bought seven hardscrabble farms totaling 1,500 acres on the lower mountainside and built over 30 structures in a mixed California/Swiss style made with stained brown native hemlock. The doors and window trim were painted a distinctive blue. There were a studio for an arts school, shops for metalworking, pottery, and woodworking, a dairy barn, a dormitory, and a library. At first the Whiteheads hoped to support the colony by making fine furniture, but pottery proved more successful. They became ceramists themselves. Bolton Brown started the painting school, but was soon replaced by **Birge Harrison**. **Hervey White**, whom Whitehead had met in Chicago as a social reformer working at Hull House, was a co-founder. Others included **Edward (Ned) Thatcher**, a metal worker; **Eva Watson-Schutze**, a photographer; and **Zulma Steele** and **Edna Walker**, both painters and crafts people.

The Whiteheads built their spacious home, **White Pines**, and entertained many prominent visitors over time: feminist author

Charlotte Perkins Gilman, New Dealer **Harry Hopkins**, educator **John Dewey**, naturalist **John Burroughs**, dancer **Isadora Duncan**, and author **Will Durant**. Poet **Wallace Stevens** visited on summer weekends when his wife was a resident ceramicist. A great beauty, she was the model whose face appeared on the old Mercury dime.

Ralph Radcliffe Whitehead was an aristocrat. Byrdcliffe was his dominion. "It was a happy, make-believe Old England. He was the Lord and master, and the artists were at his beck and call," noted Woodstock historian Alf Evers. Those who didn't care for subordinate roles didn't stay long. By 1910 it was clear his Utopian colony wouldn't match his dreams. Yet, a century later, you could say that while Byrdcliffe never really succeeded it never really failed either. Today, it's an active arts colony with 50 residents each summer. Classes are offered in woodworking, ceramics, and jewelry making. The **Byrdcliffe Theater,** built in 1902 as an art studio, later housed the Tourneau opera company and various regional theater companies over the years.

There are two good Byrdcliffe walks, one historic, one wild. Start in the theater parking lot. Outside the building there are often fliers available for a self-guided mile-long walking tour past the historic buildings. Nearby, for instance, is **Eastover**, the large house built for art faculty and later inhabited by **Chevy Chase**, **Milton and Sally Avery**, and **The Band**. **Bob Dylan** lived farther up this road in the mid-1960's in a sprawling Byrdcliffe house that had been sold into private hands. He moved across the valley to Ohayo Mountain Road, then left town for good in 1970.

Notice the upstairs sleeping porch at Eastover. Sleeping in fresh air was part of

Whitehead's health regime. He didn't allow cars or electricity into his patch of Old England until the 1920's. White Pines, the large family house, is open to the public on Saturdays in the summertime.

The **Byrdcliffe-Mount Guardian trail** starts in the theater lot and ascends past the houses into the woods that have grown up in the past century on the former farms. The

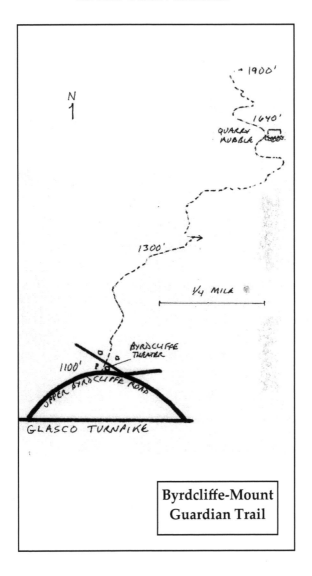

Byrdcliffe-Mount
Guardian Trail

chestnut oaks are an example of the southern hardwoods brought into the Woodstock Valley by Native Americans who burned the original forest. Mountain laurels also arrived with the fires. When they flower in June with fragrant white clusters big as popcorn balls, the forest appears to be giving itself a wedding.

You're not aiming for the top. Like many Catskill summits, Mount Guardian is flat on top with nothing to see but trees. Your destination is a rocky outcropping high on the hillside with a view over the scrub oaks into the Woodstock Valley. Though well trod, this trail isn't heavily used and has several false turns, so be prepared to pick your way. It takes an hour or more to reach the rocky outcrop from the parking lot. By the time you get there, you might feel like Bolton Brown did after finding his way through the "savage impenetrability" of the wild Catskills to discover the beauty of Woodstock below.

The Maverick
120 Maverick Road

Hervey White, a Kansas-bred, Harvard-educated, socialist reformer and bohemian writer, was a beloved figure. With mussed hair and pointed beard, he suggested "the God Pan in a pink blouse and workmen's trousers," wrote a friend at the time. "Eager, young-eyed, keen and yet dreaming, shy and yet forceful, he comes along the  open road, like one of Whitman's 'Camer12does,' always loafing and gay, and always at work on his thousand and one schemes." He dyed his own clothes, published his own poems, proudly lived in cottages that were little more than shacks, and befriended many celebrated people of the day, from social reformers such as **Clarence Darrow** and **John Dewey** to the musicians who founded the Maverick concert series.

In 1905 White left Byrdcliffe to buy his own 102-acre farm across the valley in the Hurley Patentee Woods. Slowly, a new colony developed that came to be called **The Maverick**. Years earlier he'd heard a story in Colorado of a wild white stallion called the Maverick Horse who lived free in the canyons, a tale that inspired him to compose a long poem about this horse as symbol of his aspirations. In 1924 **John Flanagan**, a talented but penniless young sculptor, took an ax to a chestnut tree and carved the wooden horse that now stands beside the concert hall stage.

After a decade, White had about 20 cottages for friends on the property and a water shortage. The well that had to be dug drilled down an unprecedented 550 feet and cost an exorbitant $1,500. To pay for it, White conceived of the Maverick Festival, an arts colony version of a medieval fair that began with afternoon picnicking and athletic contests like catching a greased pig, then continued into the night with bonfires and stage performances under electric lights meant to imitate the full moon. Everyone was encouraged to dress up: gypsies, pirates, medieval ladies and knights, Puritans, hobos. Started in 1915, these August festivals grew in renown, attracting thousands, until by the end in 1931 they'd become huge hell-raising parties where bootleggers sold their wares in the woods, a far cry from White's original vision.

Tamer, but far more enduring, the **Concert Hall** has been the Maverick's great legacy. Built in the spring of 1916 from trees on the property, it looks like a barn and feels

like a chapel, but was inspired as well by communal houses found on Fiji Island. Yet, fearing that local people already viewed colony artists as pagans, White added the peaked arches and wall patterns that suggest Gothic cathedrals. From the start, prominent musicians have played at what has become the longest running summer chamber music festival in the country. Among the early performers were **Pierre Henrotte**, concert

master for the Metropolitan Opera; **Leon Barzin**, later musical director of the New York City Ballet; and **Georges Barrère**, the most celebrated flutist in America. Adventurous composers such as **Virgil Thompson**, **Aaron Copland**, and **Henry Cowell** had pieces played here.

Cowell lived in Shady with his wife Sydney from the 1940's until his death in 1965. He was a virtuosic composer, both wildly experimental and deeply influenced by music from around the world. As a teenager in 1916, he wrote tonal cluster music that required the pianist to plant both forearms on the keyboard.

Yet no evening was like the one when young pianist **David Tudor** performed **John Cage's** 4'33" in August 1952 . Tudor turned score sheets and twice closed the piano lid to indicate the end of a movement, but never touched the keys. The composition was meant to encourage the audience to listen to natural sounds as music. Now, 4'33" may not seem like a long time, hardly more than some TV ad breaks, but by the third movement people were standing up and leaving in outrage. Depending on your aesthetics, 4'33" remains a seminal avant-garde piece of the 20th century, or a reminder that modern art lost its bearings a long time ago.

❖ ❖ ❖

The Woodstock School of Art
2470 Route 212

As part of the New Deal, the National Youth Administration chose Woodstock in 1939 as the site for a training campus for young men aged 16 to 24 to learn woodworking, stone cutting, metal-working, and wool-processing, and for young women to learn weaving. That June **Eleanor Roosevelt** drove from Hyde Park for the placing of the cornerstone for the Resident Work Center, where students built three large workshops from bluestone quarried from the property under the guidance of teachers like sculptor **Tom Penning**. Roosevelt had established a similar program, Val-Kill Industries, in Hyde Park, which ran from 1927 to 1937. At its peak the Woodstock center had 90 students. It closed in 1942 when three fourths of them left to fight in World War II.

After the war, the Art Students League found a summer school home here from 1947 to 1979. The teaching opportunities encouraged new generations of artists to move to town, including **Fletcher Martin**, **Philip Guston**, **John Pike**, and **William Pachner**.

From 1947 to 1952 a series of Woodstock Art Conferences drew such figures as **Robert Motherwell**, **Barnett Newman**, **Isamu Noguchi**, and **David Smith**, but the arts colony's national acclaim was about to be eclipsed by Abstract Expressionism and the subsequent art movements that arose elsewhere.

After the League's summer school closed in 1979, the **Woodstock School of Art**, formed by a small group of local artists in 1968 to continue teaching through the year in their own studios, grew far more ambitious and acquired the bluestone campus, which had fallen into chaos. The place had been stripped down to the lightbulbs. They repaired roofs, replaced broken windows, cleared underbrush from the lawn. Most of all, they learned how to raise money and meet budgets. They were led by **Robert Angeloch**, whose son, **Eric Angeloch**, now teaches here, as do other local artists, including **Richard Segalman, Staats Fasoldt, Donald Elder**, and **Hongnian Zhang**.

The WSA programs have grown to offer classes year-round to more than 400 people, ranging from high school students to retirees. Instructors have the freedom to teach art however they like, guaranteeing variety. Sculptors studying the human figure may even take a class in *écorché* for which they make a small skeleton. Art has gone in one radical direction after another in the past century, sometimes filling galleries with everything but paintings. But visiting these stone studio buildings to observe people patiently seated at easels, puzzling over the possibilities of color and light, is to return to the essence of Woodstock as an arts colony

The front building, originally the wood-working shop, now houses a gallery for public art exhibits by students and instructors. Behind the studios is a sculpture trail through the woods to view bluestone pieces created by a visitors from several countries, including Colum Folan of Ireland, whose works could be enchanting miniature castles for long forgotten Druidic ceremonies—if you have a pagan imagination.

These stone works remind us of others with more mysterious origins. In certain forests in Woodstock, there are stone cairns by the dozens that some people believe were left behind by Native Americans as funerary sites. There are stone mounds with stone feet like turtles. There are a pair of serpentine stone walls which end at giant boulders like rattlesnake heads. No one questions that farmers left behind miles of stone pasture walls, but these discoveries have led to speculations that the Native Americans were doing a lot more here than gathering nuts and hunting game. They may have been stacking cairns in alignment with the sun and stars. (Skeptics believe that these cairns were simply piled up by farmers to support fence posts.)

The greatest bluestone sculptor in the region had to be **Harvey Fite**, who taught at Bard College across the river in Annandale-on-Hudson. In 1938 he bought a bluestone quarry in Saugerties for raw materials. After helping to restore Mayan ruins in Honduras, he developed grander visions for his rubble pile. He named his project **Opus 40** and gave himself 40 years to complete it. When he died in 1976 by accidently driving his lawn mover off a ledge that he'd constructed—either a fitting or a macabre ending to this story of an artist and his life's work—he left behind seven acres of stone platforms and pools, terraces and hollows, ramps and stairs; a captivating place to explore—a surreal theater stage. A stone monolith stands at the top with a classic view of Overlook Mountain beyond. Opus 40 is open on weekends from late May through early October. It's located at 50 Fite Road in Saugerties.

❖ ❖ ❖

An Overlook Mountain Excursion

❖ ❖ ❖ ❖ ❖ ❖ ❖

Overlook Mountain Parking Area
Meads Mountain Road

Should Woodstock ever declare its independence as a "People's Republic," surely it would choose the saddle-backed profile of **Overlook Mountain** as the symbol on its currency. This towering southeastern corner of the Catskills Escarpment, at first called South Peak by sailors on the Hudson, has dominated the skyline and the town's consciousness from the start. **Thomas Cole**, first of the Hudson River School painters, stood on the summit on August 13, 1846 to admire the spectacular panorama that looks deep into the heart of the Catskills, but also sweeps across the Hudson Valley to take in five states and as many mountain ranges. He was the first to call the mountain Overlook instead of South Peak. He died two years later, leaving the scene unpainted. On July 31, 1873 **President Ulysses S. Grant** visited the top as a guest of the new Overlook Mountain House half-a-mile down the carriage road. He shared cigars and sat on a rock that still bears his name. (There are conflicting tales about whether or not Grant, a noted tippler, spent the previous night drunk.)

Nowadays, the 2½ mile climb up the jeep road to the summit draws everyone from trail runners to first-timers in flip flops. They're joined by young families, teenage cliques, mountain bikers, backpackers on their way to camp at Echo Lake for the night, even, on rare occasions, by paragliders who intend to sail off the cliffs in their human kite rigs. Most hikers, though, are regulars out for exercise or visitors eager to see one of the Hudson Valley's most glorious views. Be forewarned that this jeep road is a steady climb that takes an hour if you're in shape, an eternity if you're not. But no experience

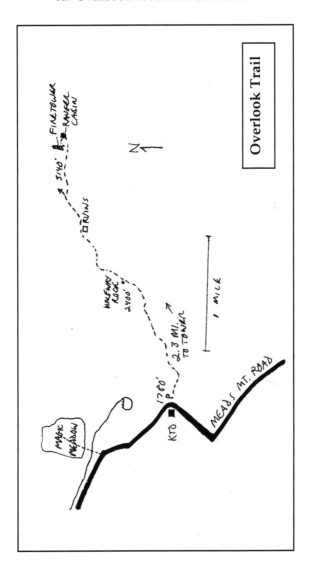

in town matches ascending the summit **fire tower** in a brisk breeze for a tingling touch of vertigo that accompanies the heavenly feeling of being on top of the world. Of course, in February that frigid climb feels like a shortcut to the North Pole.

Erected in 1950, the fire tower was used for fire spotting into the 1980's when small plane pilots took over observation duties. Now forest rangers rely on a public armed with cell phones to report fires. In the late 1990's a volunteer group restored the fire tower and the nearby ranger's cabin, which is open on weekends from Memorial Day to Columbus Day. Inside, you'll find historical photos of the old hotel, funny photos of bears, and a collection of rattlesnake skins from Overlook's most famous rare species. On certain days they're readily seen, but don't panic. They'll rattle, but haven't bitten anyone in ages. Years ago, the fire warden cooked them for dinner—now they're a protected species.

❖ ❖ ❖

The summit is a good place for a short course in forest history. From the cliffs overlooking Woodstock and the Hudson Valley, you see the forest that has blanketed the former farms and pastures of a century ago, making our region look wilder than it has in hundreds of years. There are precious few open fields left anymore. Several of the most prominent are, in fact, old dumps. Throughout these valley forests you may notice the stately white pines, a species that loves to reclaim open ground.

The gnarly trees above and below the Overlook cliffs are red oaks, one of the nut-bearing southern hardwoods along with hickories, chestnuts, and walnuts that reached the Catskills some 4,000 to 6,000 years ago as more Native Americans arrived. Before then, the area had been covered with northern hardwoods, such as maples and beeches, which still blanket the Catskills west of Woodstock. Native Americans set fires to those original forests to create the open woodlands they preferred for easier travel and hunting, plus the safety of being able to see enemies at a distance. They harvested tree nuts for themselves and hunted game animals like deer and wild turkey that also consumed acorns and nuts. The Native Americans cleared land for agriculture. They may have planted orchards of walnuts and oaks. They gave us many of the tree species commonly found in Woodstock today.

On Overlook the fires must have burned out by the cliffs. If you step behind the summit cabin into the evergreen trees, where others might take a privacy break, you've walked back 12,000 years into the boreal forest that covered the Catskills soon after the Ice Age glaciers had melted. Now the boreal forest lies in northern Canada. The surviving remnants in the Catskills are found on the highest mountains, so this patch on Overlook is a surprise. Some boreal species vanished from our region long ago, but a hardy handful remain, such as mountain ash, paper birch, red spruce, and the Christmas tree-like balsam fir found in dense thickets on mountain summits. Red spruce and balsam fire look alike. To distinguish between them, shake hands with a branch. The spruce has sharp needles, the fir soft.

Now confined to the summits, these boreal species once filled the valleys as well, and still would if not for the arrival of the northern hardwood forest about 8,000 years ago, the sugar maples and beeches that cover the

Catskills beyond the Native American burn zones. This forest type grows on the northern side of Overlook, which you may visit by starting down the trail towards Echo Lake. These large, long-lived, leafy trees have outcompeted the earlier boreal species for the best growing sites, leaving the spruces and firs to the summits with thin soils and harsh winters. Trees may look peaceful, but over time they've been invading and conquering, or losing and retreating, almost like human armies; since they lack feet, they need centuries to accomplish what we do in months.

Half a mile down from the summit stand the **hotel ruins**, towering walls as full of sky inside as out. The roof and interior were dynamited in the 1960's after two decades of falling into disrepair until they were deemed a public hazard. In fact, two earlier hotels preceded this one before they burned as well. The first, built in 1871, hosted President Grant but went up in smoke on April Fool's Day in 1875. A second constructed in 1878 did well for half a dozen years, then sat empty for decades until 1923 when it burned. Construction on this third version began in 1928 with plans for an opulent hotel with a four story lookout tower rising from the roof. Slowed by the Depression, the building was almost finished by the start of World War II, but it was ransacked during the war and left as a wreck that local children loved to explore as a haunted house into the 1960's.

The ugly **transmission tower** was built in the early 1980's for WTZA TV ("From the Tappan Zee to Albany") in Kingston, which became WRNN, which has switched to digital broadcasting, leaving the tower for other uses.

❖ ❖ ❖

Karma Triyana Dharmachakra
335 Meads Mountain Road

In 1865 **George Mead**, a silversmith from Kingston, moved his family into a farm house in this saddle then known as Wide Clove. In time it was expanded into a summer boarding house, a rambling three story structure with gables, porches, tennis courts, and a croquet lawn. Artists and intellectuals stayed here, such as **Stanford White**, the architect, and **Frederick Church**, Thomas Cole's student in the Hudson River School. Unlike the Overlook Mountain House, which had brief periods of glory between decades of neglect, the **Mead's Mountain House** ran successfully for more than a century under three generations of Meads and subsequent owners before it finally fell out of fashion, a bulky old relic with rooms for 50 in the more modern age of B&Bs and boutique motels. It wasn't an ideal building for a Tibetan Buddhist monastery, but who could question the location?

The head of the Karma Kagyu lineage of Tibetan Buddhism (a traditional practice rather than one adapted for Westerners), the

16th Karmapa, visited the United States and Canada in 1974 and enjoyed such a warm reception that he accepted the offer of a house in Putnam County from a wealthy supporter to establish a North American headquarters. But his emissaries sent over to complete the arrangements found Woodstock after one of them began leading weekly gatherings in a house on Meads Mountain Road. When the old hotel came up for sale, they bought it. In 1980 the 16th Karmapa visited to design the future shrine and other buildings for **Karma Triyana Dharmachakra**.

Construction took years, while the abbot, lamas, and practitioners used the old hotel. Some have fond memories of the place as cozy and family-like, but not Mark Rothe, KTD's executive director, who endured three winters in the mid-1980's when temperatures dropped to 20 below, chasing him from his bedroom into the bookstore for what little heat he could find. The plastic sheets draped over windows weren't the best insulation. By 1992 the shrine was completed. The handsome white buildings on a three-sided courtyard with residences for lamas and staff, and guest rooms for 44 attendees at weekend workshops opened in 2010.

No room in Woodstock is more spectacular than the main shrine. Sunlight from the cupola and wall windows flood the wooden floor and red meditation cushions. A giant gold-leafed statue of Buddha presides at one end, backed by towering maroon and glass cases holding sacred texts. His throne and everything around him is decorated with intricate gold patterns. Tapestries of holy figures hang high on the wall around the room. A visiting artist spent 18 months detailing the ceiling beams and moldings. The room is orderly yet riotous with reds, yellows, blues, and greens. To a visitor from the colonial white village below—and visitors are welcome each weekend for a tour starting at

1 pm at the bookstore—it's an eye-popping sight. Yet to practitioners nothing in the shrine room is decoration. Every object is a reminder of a teaching. The joyous extravagance simply reflects the brightness of the human mind.

The 16th Karmapa died in 1981. His reincarnation, the 17th Karmapa, escaped his Chinese handlers in Tibet at age 14 to live in exile in India, and has now visited KTD in 2008 and 2011. On his first trip, it is said, rainbows appeared wherever he went.

❧ ❧ ❧

Church of the Holy Transfiguration of Christ-on-the-Mount
325 Meads Mountain Road

George Mead built a rustic one room chapel in 1891 for his summer boarders that stands below KTD, now called **Church of the Holy Transfiguration of Christ-on-the-Mount**. In the 1930's Jane Whitehead of Byrdcliffe bought the church from the Episcopalian Diocese in Albany for a young priest from

California, **Father W. H. Francis**, whom she admired. He represented the Church of the Eastern Rites, a branch of Catholocism which recognized the Pope as a bishop rather than as a supreme authority. In the 1960's Father

Francis became known as the "hippie priest" for ministering to the young arrivals shunned by many town residents.

The door is always open, so step inside to admire the wooden interior that looks and smells as old as its years. Heed the "No Smoking" sign by the door.

❖ ❖ ❖

Magic Meadow

A short walk (less than half a mile) down the back side of the mountain will bring you to a bend in the road. Walk through the trees on the right, cross the stone foot bridge,

and head up the incline to one of Woodstock's secrets, an old cow pasture now
called the **Magic Meadow**. The huge field is
bright with laurel in June, and has been the
site over many decades of arts colony parties
(complete with piano), weddings, and hippie gatherings (with late-night drumming.)
Some say that the true Woodstock Festival—not the one in Bethel—occurred here
the night of the Harmonic Convergence in
August, 1987, when thousands gathered for
revelry around campfires and shut down the
road into town with their parked cars. To this
day, drummers gather by the dozens under
the full moon in warmer months to celebrate
the Rainbow spirit around a bonfire throw-
ing sparks at the sky.

❖ ❖ ❖

MacDaniel Road

MacDaniel Road offers classic mountain
views. The far peaks on the northern
skyline are linked by the Devil's Path, a famous Catskills trail, which roller coasters
up and down a total of six steeply-notched

mountains. Almost 26 miles long, it's considered the hardest day hike in the eastern United States. In August 2010 a trail runner set a record by finishing the path in 5 hours and 35 minutes. Mere mortals would be happy to climb one of those mountains in that time.

A Westward Excursion Through Bearsville, Lake Hill, Willow, and Mount Tremper

❖ ❖ ❖ ❖ ❖ ❖ ❖

Bearsville

Bearsville wasn't named after bears, as you might expect from seeing the wooden bear statue in the **Bearsville Complex** (291-295 Tinker Street). It was named after **Christian Baehr**, a well-educated young German immigrant who arrived in 1820 to start a sawmill, invest in a glass factory, and in 1839 open a general store that is now the apartment building on the corner of Striebel Road and Route 212. A faded antique photo of him hangs in the corner of the Bearsville Post Office. He looks like a white bearded bear.

In those years **glass factories** were Woodstock's big industry. Two glass company villages flourished along the Sawkill over the course of 50 years, the first up in what is now Keefe Hollow, the second down in Shady by Reynolds Lane, where several of the original houses remain. The factories were drawn by the forest bowl behind Overlook Mountain, a reservoir of fuel wood for their white hot furnaces. They imported sand for making glass from as far away as Perth Amboy, New Jersey to supplement what was mined at Cooper Lake. These factories were impressive sights, especially on cold winter nights when local children gathered inside by the fires to watch the glass blowers perform their magic. For the most part, they made glass for windows, but for these young admirers they'd shape glass turtles and birds as trinkets. With their powerful lungs they were also marvelous singers. The last glass factory closed in 1854, but children continued to find glass pebbles in the Sawkill into the 20th century. Today, this history has vanished, save for **Glasco Turnpike**, the Glass Company road that linked the villages to the dock on the Hudson.

❖ ❖ ❖

The **Bearsville Complex** is the legacy of **Albert Grossman**, manager of **Bob Dylan**, **Janis Joplin**, **Peter, Paul & Mary**, **The Band**, **Paul Butterfield**, and others who made Woodstock into a music mecca in the 1960's. Born in Chicago to an immigrant tailor, Grossman studied economics under Milton Friedman at the University of Chicago, but quickly became a folk music impresario in that city as an owner of the Gate of Horn, where he met and signed Odetta. Then he then followed his ambitions east. In *Chronicles*, Bob Dylan recalled their first meeting: "He looked like Sydney Greenstreet from the film *The Maltese Falcon*, had an enormous presence, always dressed in a conventional tie, and he sat at the corner table. Usually when he talked, his voice was loud like the booming of war drums. He didn't talk so much as growl." He made a fortune in part by charging ten percent more than other agents. According to legend, he earned enough from Peter, Paul & Mary's 1963 hit song, "Puff the Magic Dragon" that he could have bought himself 72 Rolls Royces.

Peter Yarrow of Peter, Paul & Mary had a mother who owned a weekend house in Woodstock. Peter brought both Grossman and Dylan for visits in the early 1960's . The town had a folk music scene, so Grossman felt at home. (In fact, the first "Woodstock Festival" was a folk festival with **Pete Seeger** and others held in 1962 on grounds now occupied by the Post Office.) Another part time Woodstocker, **Milton Glaser**, the graphic illustrator who'd done album covers for Grossman, learned of a $50,000 mansion in town that only the wealthy producer could afford. (Glaser later designed the psychedelic hair album cover for *Bob Dylan's Greatest Hits* in 1967.)

Grossman became a country squire at his house which offered a stone swimming pool, expensive antiques, fine wines, and a bacchanalian lifestyle that entertained his young clients. He dreamed of making Woodstock into a music capital with his own record label, recording studio, and fine restaurants. Rock 'n' roll stars arrived, some of them managed by Grossman, others simply drawn by the music scene. **Jimi Hendrix** stayed for several seasons in a stone house near the Ashokan Reservoir. **Van Morrison** lived off Ohayo Mountain Road with a stunning view of the Ashokan Reservoir. **Todd Rundgren** came as a 22-year protégé of Grossman's, then established his own studio in Mink Hollow, where he produced albums for acts ranging from Grand Funk Railroad to the New York Dolls. **Paul Butterfield** fronted a blues band. Brilliant but troubled **Tim Hardin** hovered on the brink of stardom.

Dylan left Grossman in 1969, starting an exodus of famous clients. But Grossman remained an intrepid mogul to the end; he suffered a heart attack on the Concorde flying to London in 1986. The **Bearsville Theater** (291 Tinker Street) that he'd envisioned opened in 1989. He lies under an oval bed of ivy in the corner of the lawn. A stone memorializes him as the "Baron of Bearsville."

That glamorous era ended after the **Rolling Stones** came to town to prepare for their 1978 world tour after releasing *Some Girls*. On local roads in the mornings drivers might see **Mick Jagger** jogging with a Jaguar trailing behind, a friendly fitness enthusiast who waved at passers-by, apparently unperturbed by the antics of his band mate, **Keith Richards**, who still led the high life and didn't appear until he hit the Joyous Lake towards midnight.

Prominent musicians still live in the area, ranging from **Donald Fagen** of Steely Dan to jazz drummer **Jack DeJohnette** to **Peter Schickele** a.k.a. P.D.Q. Bach. But you'll no longer find rock stars in the bars looking to get crazy for the night. They're more likely to be seen headlining at the Bearsville Theater in benefit concerts for local causes.

That era was also great for jazz. Founded in 1971 by **Karl Berger**, **Ingrid Sertso**, and **Ornette Coleman** the **Creative Music Studio** brought hundreds of musicians from around the world to workshop and perform together. The studio closed in 1984, but veterans such as **Marilyn Crispell** still live and play in the area.

Also in the Bearsville Complex is **WDST**, an independent FM radio station that respects the Woodstock tradition without being slavish to the past. The station staff drives around town in a painted VW bug, which, you may notice, isn't covered with

1960's-style paisley and daisies, but with aliens and flying saucers, a sly declaration of independence from hippiedom. Founded by Jerry and Sasha Gilman, WDST began broadcasting in 1980 with an eclectic mixture ranging from jazz to classical to a children's show to book readings on the air. Under new ownership it settled into a rock format in the 1990's. On Sunday mornings, you may catch the original spirit on **Doug Grunther's** "Woodstock Roundtable" talk show. In one segment he'll interview a psychic; in the next a United States Congressman.

In recent years, the late **Levon Helm**, The Band's drummer, enjoyed a silver-haired renaissance by winning Grammies for three records and by hosting **Midnight Rambles** at his modern timber frame studio barn on Plochmann Lane. The place felt like a large living room, with its bluestone fireplace and Turkish red carpet in the center where the musicians played to the crowd seated in folding chairs or standing up in the balcony. Helms's first studio barn was lost in a fire. He fought throat cancer in 1996. Two of his Band mates died much too young—**Richard**

Manuel felled by suicide at 42, **Rick Danko** by hard living at 55. Yet Helms was nothing if not a survivor. Born to an Arkansas cotton farmer, he joined a touring band right out of high school, met four Canadians who became his compatriots in the Band which played behind Bob Dylan and had their own magical run until *The Last Waltz* farewell concert of 1976. At the Ramble he took the stage and sat at his drum kit in the front corner bathed in a soft purple spotlight. He had the lean-faced charisma of an old cowboy. As the musicians played old Band favorites mixed with roadhouse blues driven by a brass section and a piano, he pounded away at the drums, all skinny shoulders and flying elbows. His smile flashed, the brightest instrument in the room. The guy couldn't have looked happier to be alive.

❖ ❖ ❖

Cooper Lake

In the 1880's the City of Kingston pushed up the Sawkill into Woodstock with dams to create reservoirs for its water supply. The first two are idyllic ponds today, one beside Sawkill Road, the other around the corner by Zena Road. They're good for windshield birding—you might see a bald eagle out on the mud flats disemboweling a fish pinned under its talons—but there's no public land for walking. A third reservoir lies in the woods between Little Deep and Big Deep. But Kingston didn't fulfill its needs until it reached **Cooper Lake**, a millpond that it drained and expanded into a reservoir in the 1920's. (Native Americans had called the pond Opdondsase.) By 1927 the others were abandoned to slowly collect silt. It takes human engineering to fill Cooper Lake. Water arrives by pipe from the stream in nearby Mink Hollow which otherwise flows west into the Beaverkill.

Cooper Lake had long been a place for pickerel fishing and ice skating. In 1924 **George Bellows** painted his most famous Woodstock scene at the lake, *The Picnic*, in which he stands by a tall fishing pole, his wife prepares a picnic blanket while his two daughters play, and his artist friend **Eugene Speicher** naps on the grass like a country bumpkin. As recently as the 1980's, secretive skinny dippers partook of the cool waters on warm summer nights.

No more. The Kingston Water Department forbids trespassing on the earthen dam. But **Cooper Lake Road** alongside the reservoir offers an enchanting walk with the same mountain views that impressed Bellows. Park on the shoulder pullover at the eastern end and enjoy 45 minutes of walking to the end and back. The deep mountain gap to the north is **Mink Hollow**, the watershed for the lake. The dominant long flank to the northwest is **Olderbark Mountain**, trailless and rarely climbed because at 3440 feet it's shy of the 3500 foot peaks pursued by the Catskill 3500 Club. Believe us, it's a tougher climb than many that are taller.

If you're lucky, you'll see the **Cooper Lake Whale**. We've only seen it once, a tall spout of water on an early spring day when loons flew overhead. Don't believe the other local legend about the wooden remains of a Viking ship having been found on the shore.

❧ ❧ ❧

If you enjoy walking country roads, let us suggest two more, **Plochmann Lane** near the village and **Sickler Road** off Route 212 in

Willow. Both are two miles long and wide enough that you won't feel intimidated by cars. Plochmann Lane starts by houses behind the Woodstock Playhouse and ends with meadow views of Overlook Mountain. Sickler Road skirts the edge of the Beaverkill Valley, nestling you in a Catskills kingdom.

Cooper Inn
3836 Route 212

Near the eastern end of Cooper Lake on Route 212 stands a white house with a double verandah that was William M. Cooper's tavern in the 1830's, a gathering spot for land tenants who seethed at their absentee landlords, the Livingstons, who held much of Woodstock under the Hardenbergh Patent granted before the Revolution. In the Catskills the growing resistance became known as the Anti-Rent Wars led by Downrenters, as in "Down with the Rent." Disguised as Indians, a group in Woodstock tarred and feathered a landlord's agent in March, 1845, infuriating the authorities who dispatched a militia of 100 men to struggle through the snow and rugged terrain to arrest some of the "Indians," including William M. Cooper.

The Downrenters lost this skirmish but won in Albany a year later when the state legislature reformed the land ownership system. A newly elected Anti-Rent governor pardoned those who'd been arrested. Many tenants bought their farms within the next decade, including the ancestors of families still recognized in the area today, such as the **Shorts**, **Shultises**, **Hasbroucks**, **De-Walls**, **Riseleys**, **Rickses**, **Happys**, **Lashers**, **Winnes**, **Duboises**, **Hogans**, **Eltings**, **Van de Bogarts**, and **Lewises**.

Mink Hollow

Near the corner of **Mink Hollow Road** and Route 212 stood the home and tavern of **Captain Elias Hasbrouck** a Revolutionary war hero who was elected Woodstock's first supervisor in 1787 upon hosting the first town meeting at his house. He served two terms before dying in office in 1791. At that time this area, known as Little Shandaken, was a budding crossroads thanks to the road

that had been built north across the notch
into the Schoharie Creek Valley in 1783. That
road lasted until the advent of cars in the
1920's. Now the pavement ends at a trail-
head parking lot. The **Mink Hollow trail** fol-
lows the old road, now eroded to jumbled
rocks in some stretches, for 2 ½ miles to the
notch between two mountains on the Devil's
Path, Sugarloaf to the east (right), Plateau
to the west (left). If you've hiked Overlook
Mountain, this trail is a nice complement:
no views, but fewer people and a peaceful
immersion in the classic Catskills northern
hardwoods forest.

Mink Hollow wasn't named after the animal, but after a freed slave named Mink who
lived in the valley in the 1890's.

❊ ❊ ❊

Willow

Woodstock Farm Animal Sanctuary
35 Van Wagner Road

How times have changed. Once Woodstock
had farm pastures everywhere. Now you
have to search to find cows at, say, the end

of Keefe Hollow Lane. Instead of farms, there's the **Woodstock Farm Animal Sanctuary**. Don't expect a petting zoo, hay rides, or nostalgic stories of farm life. The sanctuary means to disabuse you of any innocence about factory farming. You'll see a wooden crate where a veal calf spends its short life with its head cradled between V-shaped slats. Also, a metal cage where five crowded hens have no room to flap their wings. Yet these animal rights activists have the good sense to let the animals be their own best emissaries, more than 200 chickens, ducks, turkeys, rabbits, sheep, goats, pigs, and cows that all have names and often frightful histories of evading slaughter houses. To gaze into their eyes is to feel the empathy you'd have for a pet.

This sanctuary is a place for happy endings, says **Jenny Brown**, who moved to Woodstock full time in 2004 and soon married her partner **Doug Abel**. They'd purchased what was locally known as the *Wizard of Oz* house, a blue Victorian with a square turret rising between gabled windows at the far end of a hay field. They toned down the color to teak stained. They've converted the field into a farm with half a dozen sheds and barns, all paid for by fundraising. Both have backgrounds in TV and film—she started in animal rights by doing undercover videos for PETA; he's a film editor for Comedy Central, film maker Errol Morris, and others—so they're media savvy. Chrissie Hynde has played a benefit concert at the farm. So has Moby. In the barn Jenny introduced us to Judd Hirsch's hermaphroditic goat.

From April 1st through October 31st the farm is open to visitors from 11 am to 4 PM on Saturdays and Sundays. Thousands visit each summer. (Now a nearby B&B in an 1850's farmhouse is open year round.) The tours are informative yet fun, a chance to give a pig a belly rub and think about switching to Fakin' Bacon for breakfast.

The northern end of **Silver Hollow Road** brings you down into one of the prettiest horse farm valleys in the region. By now, you're out of Woodstock into Greene County, but you'll feel like you're in Little Vermont.

Mount Tremper

Zen Mountain Monastery
871 Plank Road

On a country drive one spring day in 1980, **John Daido Loori**, then a Zen student in Los Angeles, happened upon an intriguing Norwegian castle-like building fallen into disrepair. Built in the 1930's as a Catholic retreat with bluestone and oak trees from the property, the place had later been a Lutheran day camp but now sat dark and unused. The intrepid Daido Loori, a Navy veteran, pushed open a basement window and hopped down into a spacious room with a stone fire place and wooden ceiling beams, and knew that he'd found something special. That the building sat by the confluence of two rivers backed by a mountain made this a providential location for a spiritual retreat.

He bought the place on a handshake and set about creating the **Zen Mountain Monastery**, the Catskills center for the Mountains and Rivers Order of Zen Buddhism which has adapted this 2,500 year old practice from Japan for Americans. Some 30 people live here, including monks who have taken lifetime vows and lay residents who stay for a month or a year at a time. Almost every weekend workshops are held for guests. On Wednesday evenings at 7:30 (6:30 in winter) and Sunday mornings at 9, the public is invited to join in meditation services. On Wednesdays cookies are offered afterwards. On Sundays people stay for a community lunch.

Half the building looks like a bluestone church; a sculpture of Christ is embedded in the towering triangular wall at one end between two tall narrow windows deliberately shaped like candles. The wooden portion of the structure employs a Scandinavian Arts and Crafts style popular at great camps and summer resorts early in the 20th century. The wrought iron hinges and door handles decorated with acorns, butterflies, birds, and other forest elements cast in iron add a playful touch. The former church sanctuary now has rows of black pillows for seated meditation. Everyone adheres to the daily routine that includes meditation, work practice, and Buddhist study. The property has outbuildings for retreats, plus a cemetery where Daido Loori's remains were interred in 2009. Thousands now use this building every year. Not one enters through the basement window.

Parks, Preserves, and Beautiful Places

Kenneth L. Wilson Public Campground & Day Use Area
859 Wittenberg Road

Assembled from old farms and opened in 1979, this state property leads a dual life. From mid-May through Columbus Day, it's a campground with trailer and tent sites; a boathouse that has rentals for paddling on the pond; a picnic area with tables and grills; a horseshoe pit; the only thing missing is swimming, no longer permitted because it stirs up silt in the pond. The rest of the year, when no fees are charged but the gates remain open, Woodstockers treat the place like a town park, a idyllic spot for **walking, snow shoeing, cross country skiing,** or **mountain biking** on the campground roads and the four trails that loop around the rolling forested terrain. Each loop is a mile or so long. A nature trail leads past beaver meadows and ponds.

The most unusual sight are **kettles**, large smooth craters left by melting Ice Age glaciers. You'll find one along the campground C Loop between tent sites #52 and #54, a round pit where a large slab of ice was left buried as the glacier receded. When it melted, it left this bowl. Mountain bikers have been known to treat this rare feature as a stunt track, racing up and down the curved banks.

Birders like this park. In May, it may be the best spot in town to watch migrating **warblers** pass through the area in their yellow flecked splendor because it has both forest and field habitats. Earlier in spring, **American woodcocks** fly at twilight above the field in one of nature's strangest mating rituals. First you listen for the males to make

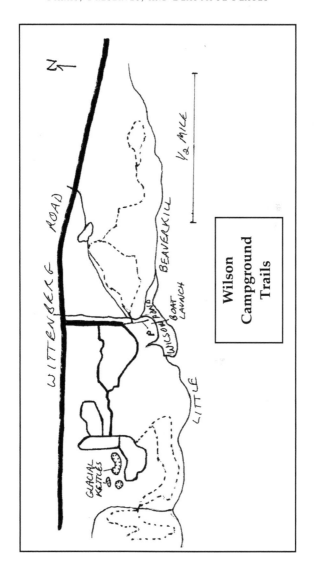

Wilson Campground Trails

a telltale electric buzzer sound somewhere off on the grounds. Then, if you're lucky, you spot them flying overhead in the fading light in crazy, ferris wheel-like patterns. Then they top out and swoop down with whistling wings. All this to impress the ladies.

These woods are also one of the few places where you can still see **ruffed grouse**. They have their own strange ritual. To establish their territory in spring, the males stand on a fallen log and thump their wings against their chests, making a sound like that of an outboard motor starting up but then petering out. Having written a poetry book, *My Late Mother as a Ruffed Grouse*, Will Nixon is partial to these birds.

❊ ❊ ❊

Kenneth L. Wilson, a popular "peoplitician," was Woodstock Town Supervisor from 1944 to 1953, then State Assemblyman from 1953 to 1969. He advocated for the creation of this campground.

❊ ❊ ❊

Another state parcel worth visiting for longer (three miles minimum, seven miles total) but still relatively easy walking trails is **Onteora Lake** on Route 28 in the Town of Kingston. The sign is easy to miss. (It's on the north side across the road from Brad's Barns at 903 Route 28.) The gravel turnoff road leads into a surprisingly serene narrow lake that offers good paddling and good fishing for pickerel, bass, and sunfish. The trails in this area pass among 19th century bluestone quarry sites that left rubble piles now spotted with lichen. Back in the heyday of quarrying, before cheaper Portland cement replaced bluestone in the 1880's, convoys of rock-laden wagons rolled out of these hills down to Hudson River docks, where workers carved them for sidewalks or curbs. As you explore, remain alert to the trail makers; unmarked old roads run through these woods that can get you lost for hours. One may have been the first route to connect Kingston to Woodstock, now completely forgotten.

Onteora, "Land of the Sky," is a common Catskills name. The Onteora School District includes much of Woodstock. In the past tempers have flared over the Onteora High School's choice of an Indian as its mascot. But Onteora is a word coined by a white man in 1843 who combined the Iroquoian

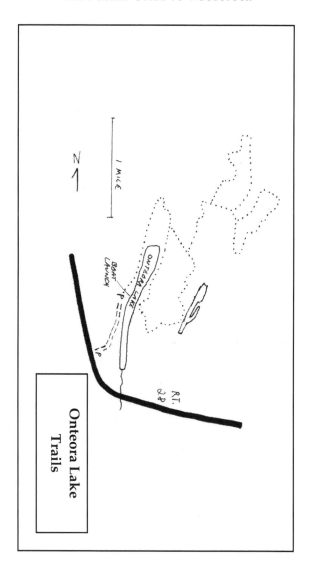

Onteora Lake
Trails

root words for mountain and sky. He didn't mean to deceive people, but the region has embraced the "Indian" name ever since.

❖ ❖ ❖

Sloan Gorge Preserve
Stoll Road

In 1970, after the death of his beloved wife, **Allan Edward Sloan**, a Woodstock portrait artist who'd painted pastels of children at Saks Fifth Avenue during the holiday seasons, bought an 88-acre property near the town border in hopes that relatives from Cleveland might move east and build there. They never did. Was it because he jokingly called the property Snake Acres? In 1998, before dying, he gave the property to the **Woodstock Land Conservancy**, which wisely renamed it **Sloan Gorge Preserve** after the dramatic, if seemingly shrunken to three-quarters sized, gorge that may be explored on a 1 ½ mile loop trail. The two iron bridge trusses that stand as a gateway to the trail are family legacies made in 1887 by the King Bridge Company, the source of the Sloans' wealth. Of Zenas King, who founded the

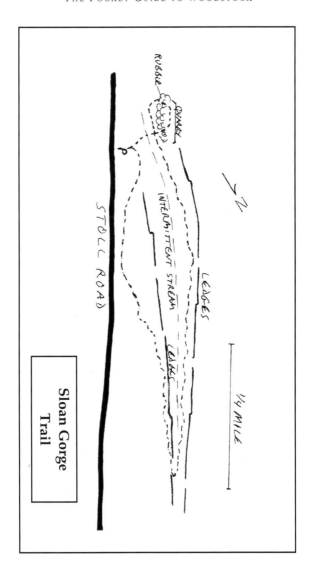

Sloan Gorge Trail

company in 1858, a biographer once wrote, "What Bell is to the telephone, Morse to the telegraph, Fulton to the steamboat, and Goodyear to the vulcanized rubber industry, Zenas King is to the science of building iron bridges."

Not far on the trail you'll reach the loose rubble piles left by bluestone quarries in the early 1900's. There were large commercial quarries, such as California Quarry on Overlook Mountain, but hundreds of smaller ones like these. A farmer who wanted a chimney or a stone foundation might well quarry his own property.

❖ ❖ ❖

What's unique at this preserve is the **geology trail** that **Robert Titus** has created to tell the story revealed by these cliffs. The Catskills may look like mountains. Anyone who has taken the trouble to join the Catskill 3500 Club by climbing all 35 peaks over 3,500 feet tall will share daunting tales of bushwhacking up to rugged trailless summits.

But Titus, a Hartwick College professor who writes popular books and columns about Catskills geology, would like to turn our view upside down.

Almost 400 million years ago, the Catskills were, in fact, a vast river delta akin to the Ganges Delta of today, catching the runoff silt from the Acadian Mountains to the east that stood as tall as the Himalayas. Our bluestone is petrified river beds. The horizontal lines that make Catskill sandstone so distinctive are layers of river bottoms laid down by time. The red layers also found here are the remains of tropical soils during those warmer eons.

The collision of Africa and North America nearly 400 million years ago pushed up the folds of the Appalachian mountains as the Catskill Delta formed. When the continents slid apart 90 million years later, the pressure release caused bedrock fracturing, leaving smooth vertical walls, called joints, still seen in Sloan Gorge today.

Then came the Ice Age glaciers. What had once been a tropical delta looked more like Antarctica. Only Slide Mountain at over 4,000 feet was tall enough to rise above the ice sheets. Some 14,000 years ago, as the last of these towering glaciers melted away, the Catskills got their final geological sculpting. Sloan Gorge was carved by waters pouring off the glaciers, a roaring cataract in contrast to the placid scene of today with its quiet trickles and swamp pools spread along the bottom. Thoe raging torrents are long gone. Now Sloan Gorge offers a perfect pocket of serenity.

The Woodstock Land Conservancy has helped preserve more than a dozen places in town. The most beloved is the **Zena Cornfield** with its picturesque view of Overlook Mountain photographed countless times. It's located on Zena Road near Route 212.

Settlers farmed the cornfield as early as 1720, as had Native Americans before them, and early militias used it as a training ground. In 1989, in the midst of a building boom, the property came up for sale. The fledgling Conservancy, having $2,000 to its name, nonetheless signed a contract to buy it for $160,000, fearing that fancy houses would fill the parcel if they didn't act. In eight weeks they raised the money by inspiring many Woodstockers to a sense of loyalty to this piece of ground. Since then, people have primarily appreciated the cornfield through their windshields while driving by. There is a picnic table, though, at the edge by Gitnik

Road if you'd like to stop and stare a while.

The field has grown hay, not corn, for decades. When asked about reverting, the Conservancy mutters dark words about pesticides.

If you continue driving on **Zena Road**, you'll travel into Woodstock's earliest days. Beside the serpentine road curves is a private house that has preserved a grist mill from before the 1750's. The crossroads at Zena Road and **Sawkill Road** was the first settled hamlet in the area, called **Waghkonck**. The stone **Van Etten House** at the corner was built in the early 18th century. Behind the fire house is Woodstock's first cemetery. Many of the headstones have eroded to smooth bluestone, but several flags are placed each year for veterans of the American Revolution.

Yankeetown Pond
Glenford-Wittenberg Road

At **Yankeetown Pond** the shoreline is in private hands, so you can't walk here, but it's still worth a stop and look from the roadway because the spot is so gorgeous. Sawmills appeared at the outlet by the 1790's. In the 1940's and 1950's Tom Shultis operated one powered by a water turbine. Today a beaver dam lies atop a human dam, proof that great minds think alike, or at least that rodent teeth and poured concrete can achieve the same ends.

Yankeetown Pond has the vegetation of both an **acidic bog** and a **neutral lake**. Bog mats of sphagnum moss and leatherleaf plants have grown out from the shoreline and created several quaking islands. True bogs in the Catskills may up to 8,000 years old, preserving plant debris in highly acidic environments that prevent organic decay, but the bog mats at Yankeetown Pond are only 20 to 30 years old. Nor is the water acidic. Water lilies grow in the shallows, while cat tails and button bush appear by the shore, plants typical of lakes.

The bog has encouraged local lore like that of the ghost of Sebastian Rhinehart, who came home from the Civil War and lived on an island in the pond in a dugout shelter. His wife didn't want to live underground like a marsupial, so she left him for another man. The story has it that Sebastian Rhinehart murdered their daughter, although he was never charged with the crime, and his bones lie on one of those bog islands.

There's a pullover spot on **Pond Road** just off the **Glenford-Wittenberg Road** (an old Indian path) where you can stop and admire Yankeetown Pond. Twice a year you may even go forth across the water. For a month in the spring before the lily pads grow too thick, **kayakers** put in from this spot to paddle out past the peninusula point to the wilder end of the lake where beaver huts proliferate like mud and stick pyramids. In winter **ice skaters** and **cross country skiers** arrive after the lake has frozen. You might even find the peace sign carved in the ice.

❖ ❖ ❖

Ohayo Mountain Road

Ohayo Mountain Road starts in the village at the intersection with **Millstream** and **Tannery Brook Roads** at **Sully's Bridge**. In late 19th century Dan Sully was a popular American theater performer who started as a circus acrobat and became a stage star known for playing Irish priests on Broadway and around the country. In 1886 he married a Woodstock native and moved with her to Mink Hollow. He rehearsed his plays in the Methodist Church, and took up farming and operating sawmills, one of which stood near this bridge. His drama *The Old Mill Stream* about conflicts over a sawmill in Mink Hollow ran on Broadway. But the 1908 song, "Down by the Old Mill Stream," was written by somebody enamored with a river in Ohio.

Not far up Ohayo Mountain Road, within sight of the Sawkill, a picket fort was established during the Revolutionary War by Woodstock's leading citizen, **Elias Hasbrouck**, who billeted a company of rangers there to protect the hamlet against raids by the British and their Mohawk allies.

Halfway up the mountain on the left is a house once rented by **The Band**. (Their practice sessions were so loud the neighbors complained.) A little farther up, **Bob Dylan** owned a house hidden from view by a long driveway. Ohayo Mountain Road crosses the top and descends into Glenford on the other side. There are fine views of the **Ashokan Reservoir**. This area was home to some of Woodstock's witches.

On Spencer Road, on the Glenford side, lived folk artist **Clarence Schmidt**, who spent almost 30 years from 1940 constructing his "Miracle on the Mountain" or "crazy castle," (depending on your tastes) from castoff materials on five acres of inherited land. What started as a single cabin grew into a junkyard chalet seven stories tall; mismatched windows faced every which way. He also liked to wrap things in tin foil. Once offered $40,000 for a piece of this artwork, he scoffed. His oeuvre burned to the ground in 1968.

Rock star **Maria Muldaur** also lived on Spencer Road.

❖ ❖ ❖

The Ashokan Reservoir

Built between 1907 and 1916, the **Ashokan Reservoir** was a) a tactical political maneuver as a way for New York City to evade land speculators who'd bought potential reservoir sites closer to the city, b) an enduring source of resentment among the people from the seven communities that were forced to move houses, churches, and cemeteries ahead of the flooding, c) an engineering marvel as the largest reservoir in the world at the time, d) the source of 500 million gallons of New York City's drinking water each day, e) the place for a spectacular panoramic view of the Catskills, f) and more. The reservoir is 12 miles long and has two separate basins divided by a weir under a bridge. There are 40 miles of shoreline open to fishermen who have permits to use rowboats. During severe droughts when the water level drops and the shorelines become dirt flats, ghost villages appear at the bottom.

The Ashokan exerts an influence in Woodstock. In 1996 New York City reached an agreement with towns in its Catskill watershed, which includes five more reservoirs, to take steps to preserve water quality so that the City won't need to build a multi-billion dollar filtration plant. In some communities the City has built sewage treatment plants. In Woodstock the City has become the largest landowner in the western half of town, buying every large parcel it can in order to preserve forests in the Ashokan watershed. Hikers and mountain bikers hope that these lands will eventually offer miles of new trails.

Most of the reservoir is closed to the public. **Route 28A** offers spectacular views at the eastern end, as does the **Reservoir Road** bridge across the weir south of Route 28 in Shokan. Two miles east of the bridge on Route 28A, there's a side road to a **parking area** where you may join strollers, Rollerbladers, and others on the mile-plus walkway built atop the earthen dam. Here you may enjoy the spectacular panorama in the fresh air, rather than through the windshield. At the end of this pedestrian drag strip you may turn around or cross the bridge intersection to continue on for another two miles on a dam road closed after 9/11. In the spring **bald eagles** have nested in a shoreline pine tree within sight of the road.

❖ ❖ ❖

Once decimated by DDT that caused them to lay egg shells too thin to survive, bald eagles have staged a dramatic comeback since 1976 when wildlife biologists first brought chicks from Alaska and elsewhere to raise and release in New York State. By the early 1990's these regal fish-eating birds had begun nesting on the Ashokan shoreline and leading soap opera lives. One May an invading female chased the resident female out of her nest, killed her chick and later attempted to kill her. The resident male, returning with a fish meal to discover that his partner had changed, issued terrible cries but ultimately paired up with her the next year. This time the invader got her comeuppance. In March a new intruder chased her and the male off the nest long enough to expose their incubated egg to the cold. She returned to sit on that egg until June 5th, almost two months after it should have hatched. The next year the pair succeeded with two fledglings. Of course, the very first pair of bald eagles to nest and breed in New York State under this program had been a brother and a sister, so the triumphant return of this endangered species has been a tabloid story from the start.

❧ ❧ ❧

Two Classic Waterfalls
Kaaterskill Falls and Plattekill Falls

To see memorable waterfalls, you'll need to drive north from town. The **Catskill Escarpment**—the mountain profile known as the **Wall of Manitou** that looks so imposing from the Thruway—is cut by two steep cloves. Each has water pouring down. Otherwise they're opposites, one grand and famous, the other wild and half-forgotten. One has spectacle, the other mystery.

❧ ❧ ❧

Kaaterskill Clove, the northern one, is served by Route 23A, a modern highway connecting the Hudson Valley with the mountaintop communities of Tannersville and Hunter. Halfway up Route 23A above a hairpin turn is a parking area for the trail, which starts back at the turn and leads half a mile up to the base of **Kaaterskill Falls**, the Catskill's most famous sight. The trail is well trod but steep in spots, so give yourself time. At the head of this valley shaded with hemlocks, you'll see what the fuss has been about, New York State's tallest waterfall. The stream pours off the top ledge to drop 175 feet past a rounded amphitheater eroded into softer rock behind the falls. The water pools on a second ledge before cascading another 85 feet down the rocks. In winter towering ice cones fed by the spray grow up from the bottom.

(Be careful! There are many accidents here. See page 142 of our book, **Walking Woodstock**, for our terrible misadventure one pretty March day.)

Kaaterskill Falls became famous in the 1820's. Up above the falls at South Lake less than two miles away, the **Catskill Mountain**

House opened in 1824, inaugurating the age of mountain hotels that lasted over a century. *The Pioneers* by **James Fenimore Cooper** advertised the falls as "the best piece of work" yet "met with in the woods." In 1826 **Thomas Cole** painted *Falls of Kaaterskill*, a brooding masterpiece of American art which renders the scene as the dark autumnal gate of the American wilderness guarded by a lone Indian warrior. Even then, Cole was mythologizing our vanishing frontier.

In July, 1844 young **Henry David Thoreau** stayed at a guest house built by sawmill owners on the stream above the falls. The following summer, writing his first diary entry at Walden, he fondly compared his new home to that guest lodge "high-placed, airy and perfumed, fit to entertain a travelling god."

Kaaterskill Falls always draws crowds, so don't expect Thoreauvian solitude. To escape the hordes, try **Platte Clove**, the southern notch in the Catskill Escarpment. Unlike Route 23A in Kaaterskill Clove, **Platte Clove Road** (Route 16) is a narrow seasonal road, closed in winter and not one to race up or down at any time. There are rusted car hulks down the steep embankments that didn't make it. The clove has a series of water-falls—10? 14? 18? Take your pick from different guidebooks—but they're not accessible from the bottom without trespassing. We recommend driving beyond the top a short distance to the **Platte Clove Preserve** open to the public by the Catskill Center. Look for the red cottage down to the left that is used in summers for an artists' retreat.

An old hotel road from here to Overlook Mountain is marked as a hiking trail. A separate path leads from near the cottage down the steep hillside to the secluded base of **Plattekill Falls**, a wet and mossy rock face 70 feet tall. An artist staying at the red cottage once told us that while she was working at her easel below the falls she looked up to see a black bear ambling across the top. She was too nervous to add the visitor to her painting

.

❖ ❖ ❖ ❖ ❖ ❖

Outdoor Fun

❖ ❖ ❖ ❖ ❖ ❖ ❖

Walking

From the start, boarding houses promoted walking to their summer guests. The Overlook Mountain House offered extensive trails and bridle paths in the 1870's and anointed every rock and crevice with an important names like "Rip Van Winkle Cave." (In truth, Rip slept in Kaaterskill Clove, well north of here.) In the 19th century pedestrianism was a science, not merely putting one foot in front of the other. "There are fashions and airs of pedestrians as in dressing, and not one lady in ten practices it correctly for health or true pleasure," scolded one hotel's brochure from 1889. "There is the swaggering air, the erect gait, the contented tread of aristocracy, the quiet pace, the shuffling step, the stoop or the halt pace—and few walk correctly."

Today, we're more democratic about walking styles. But we've ceded too much to automobiles. At the Chamber of Commerce & Arts information booth, the second most popular question after "Where was the concert held?" is "Where can we go for a walk?" Oddly, for a town in which a third of the land is protected for conservation, Woodstock has only a handful of public trails. There may be miles upon miles of old woods roads through the forests, but so many cross private lands that you'll need a local resident to lead you on a private tour. Fortunately, the public trails that Woodstock does have are worth exploring. They're described elsewhere in the book. For a reminder:

For easy walks on relatively flat terrain that take an hour or less, visit the **Comeau Property** (page 38), **Sloan Gorge Preserve** (page 148), and **Wilson Campground** (page 143). **Onteora Lake** has longer trail loops that may take a few hours (page 145).

Overlook Mountain (page 107) is a must if you don't mind climbing. On **Mount Guardian** (page 95) you'll escape the crowds. **Mink Hollow** (page 133) doesn't have views but immerses you in the classic Catskills forest.

Are you ready for longer hikes? Beyond Woodstock in the central and northern Catskills, there's an extensive trail system over many of the mountains. There are good hiking guidebooks, such as the Adirondack Mountain Club's *Catskill Trails* by our friends Carol and David White. The New York-New Jersey Trail Conference set of Catskill Trails maps is essential. An easier hike that we favor is the 1 ½ mile trail up to **Giant Ledge**, where you'll be among the high peaks without marching for hours to get there. The **North/South Lake State Campground** area has trail loops as well as magnificent Hudson Valley views. It's the site of the **Catskill**

Mountain House, the most famous of the region's hotels.

For a break from the mountains, drive down to the Hudson. A mile and a half from the Saugerties village center stands the **Saugerties Lighthouse** built in 1869 on a point in the river. It's reached by a half mile nature trail through sandy forest and marsh reeds. The trail floods at high tide so be careful with timing. (The parking area is at 168 Lighthouse Drive.) About two miles south of Saugerties in the hamlet of Glasco is the **Falling Waters Preserve** owned by the Dominican Sisters of Sparkill. This bucolic retreat has nearly two miles of trails on carriage roads or down by the riverside. In the 19th century a giant ice house at this site stored 10,000 tons of ice harvested from the river that would be shipped to New York City in warmer months.

Finally, across the Kingston Rhinecliff Bridge and half a mile north on River Road (County Route 103) is **Poets' Walk**, an estate property that has kept its Romantic landscape design from 1849. The carriage path over the rolling hay-covered terrain passes through "outdoor rooms" marked by tree rows. A wooden pavilion stands at the crest with a spectacular view of the Catskill Escarpment. You'll see why Hudson River sailors called Overlook Mountain "South Peak." Seen from this perspective, it's the corner of the Wall of Manitou.

❖ ❖ ❖

Bicycling

Step into **Overlook Mountain Bikes** (93 Tinker Street) and you'll feel as if you're in a rock climbing shop in New Paltz or a ski shop in Hunter. There's an outdoorsy, jockish, gearhead atmosphere along with the smell of tires on bikes hung from the ceiling. Owner **Billy Denter** believes that we're in one of the premier regions of the country for both **road riding** and **mountain biking**, a sport pioneered in the late 1970's on Mount Tamalpais north of San Francisco that reached the Catskills in the mid-1980's.

You wouldn't know it to look at it while driving up Route 28 from Kingston, but those wooded ridges up behind the gas marts and shopping strips on the north side are a local mountain biking mecca. More than 30 miles of trails on former bluestone quarry lands now protected by the Catskill Forest Preserve may be reached from **Onteora Lake** off Route 28 or up on **Jockey Hill** via side roads. In places the iron-rung wagon wheels cut grooves in the bedrock on the quarry roads that can still be seen today.

For shorter trails, there's Wilson Campground; for a mountain, Overlook.

Overlook Mountain Bikes also has a flier for three suggested road rides in town: a four miler, a 14-plus miler, and a 20 miler. The first two take you east out of the village, either on a shorter loop via Plochmann Lane, Glasco Turnpike, and Rock City Road back to the village, or on a longer loop that includes Chestnut Hill Road, Van Dale Road, Zena Road, John Joy Road, and Glasco Turnpike. The 20-mile loop heads west from Bearsville on Wittenberg Road (County Route 40) and returns on Route 212 with pretty alternative routes along Sickler Road and Cooper Lake Road. For those who want a 50 miler, ask at the bike shop.

If Overlook Mountain Bikes is for

gearheads, then **The Old Spokes Home** in a barn behind Changes (19 Tinker Street) is for Thoreauvian simplifiers. Owner **Michael Esposito** arrived in Woodstock in 1967 fresh from a youthful career as a rock 'n' roller with the Blues Magoos, a group who enjoyed a #5 hit. He fell in love with the village as "Mayberry LSD." (Though the Blues Magoos were the first big psychedelic band, he didn't partake himself, spending his free time while on tour collecting rare guitars from pawn shops.) For five years, Esposito lived in a cabin he built for his own Thoreauvian retreat. In time, he began playing bass for a local band and repairing and remaking bikes in the barn. He hasn't driven a car since 1977, long after giving up his rock star's Jaguar XKE. He sells $25 bikes to the Mexicans who work in restaurant kitchens, Woodstock's hidden labor force.

❖ ❖ ❖

Swimming the Sawkill

A century ago the Sawkill's swimming holes were popular meeting grounds for summer arts students; some brought soap to bathe, since they rented sleeping space in barns. In the 1920's these bohemians grew so numerous that the City of Kingston, fearing for the health of its water supply, took legal action to kick people out of the stream, but failed after Woodstockers held a "swim-in" to protest in 1922. So Kingston built a six mile pipe from its Cooper Lake reservoir under the village to avoid the turmoil. Decades later, hippies restored the bohemian practice of skinny dipping, still fondly remembered by Baby Boomers no longer so quick to strip out of their clothes. Some swimming holes of the past have been closed by surly landowners along the stream banks. But four remain as popular as ever. The first two are right in the village.

Tannery Brook Road crosses Sully's Bridge before intersecting Ohayo Mountain Road (to the right) and Millstream Road (to the left). Just upstream is a popular spot where the stream staircases down bedrocks. Not far downstream beside Millstream Road is a second hangout at the confluence with Tannery Brook. On hot summer days children and teenagers who walk from the village take ownership of these swimming holes.

❖ ❖ ❖

A short drive out of the village are **Big Deep** and **Little Deep**. Take Route 212 east for 1 ½ miles from the village center towards Saugerties. On the right there's a sign for **Casablanca Lane**. That's no coincidence. Hollywood screenwriter **Howard Koch**, who shared an Oscar for co-writing the screenplay for *Casablanca*, lived on this lane for many years after being blacklisted in the early 1950's. A Kingston native, he'd gotten his start by writing the radio script for Orson Welles' *War of the Worlds*.

Just after Casablanca Lane on the right is an unmarked gravel driveway into the parking area for Big Deep, a beloved swimming hole where you'll get away from traffic. After parking, walk the woods road blanketed with pine needles to a natural pool which has a silt beach beneath the hemlock trees.

Little Deep isn't so far downstream, but it's best to drive so as not to trespass by houses above the stream embankment. Continue east on Route 212, then turn right on Zena Road. Zena Cornfield is on the left. On the right before the bridge is a shoulder parking area, where a trail leads into the swimming pool beside bedrocks that provide streamside seating. This path continues for a pleasant ten-minute walk to an impressive stone dam built for one the Kingston reservoirs abandoned in 1927. Above the dam lies a bucolic marsh.

❖   ❖   ❖

Tubing

Is tubing outdoor recreation? Or grown up silliness? Either way, it can be lots of fun. In summer **Phoenicia** becomes the tubing capital. Several companies outfit floaters with bombproof inner tubes and life jackets, then bus them a few miles out of town to bob and wallow and bump down through the Esopus rapids. Be forewarned, the water may be cold. A soaking wet cotton tee shirt can chill you to goosebumps even on a bright summer day. In winter Hunter Mountain offers offers snow tubing on a lower slope. The one skill you need for tubing is the ability to laugh.

❖   ❖   ❖

Winter Sledding and More

The dead of winter brings the doldrums to Woodstock. Shops and restaurants close for post-holiday vacations. The ski traffic to Belleayre or Hunter largely bypasses the village. Events listings shrink because promoters and performers won't risk weather cancellations. The sun barely climbs out of the trees before sinking again after lunch. The snowbirds leave for Florida. The locals look frumpy in padded layers of long johns and sweaters and winter expedition-sized coats. Older people worry about slipping on ice. The auto body repair shops do a booming business after storms. Everybody wonders how much longer this can go on. Then a March blizzard drops twenty inches of snow up in the hollows west of town. SUVs that make it down to the village look like igloos on wheels.

The antidote is to dress warmly and think like a kid again. Treat the snow as a free gift from the skies. **Sledding Hill** draws children and parents to the sloped meadow on Route 212 across the road from the Post Office. **Yankeetown Pond** attracts ice skaters and cross country skiers. A cold winter may inspire a bonfire party out on the ice. Once you've tried winter hiking, you might find it your favorite season of the year. Sweeping views appear from hillsides that would be cloaked in summer foliage. The **Overlook** trail is popular in winter, though you may want ice cleats for your boots because the carriage road gets very slick. Snow shoeing is great fun once the snow is deep enough. **Wilson Campground** is a good spot for cross country skiing. Birders may find snow buntings at the **Ashokan Reservoir** and overwintering ducks like mergansers and buffleheads at **Cooper Lake** and the old reservoir ponds in Zena. Even if you're not an outdoors buff, don't give up hope. Valentine's Day often inspires an erotic art show somewhere in the region.

❖ ❖ ❖

Farewell, For Now

To Jeff Moran, a former town supervisor who in denim jeans and fleece vest resembles a lean and smiling L.L. Bean cowboy, the secret of Woodstock's charm lies in the ancient Chinese precepts of feng shui, according to which our village sits in an ideal location. We have a mountain to the north for protection. Open terrain to the south for sunlight and expansiveness. Hills to the west as a break against storms. Egress to the east in the form of the Thruway and the Hudson River. In China, such locations aren't rare because the mountains run east and west, allowing many settlements in southern facing valleys. But in North America the great mountain ranges run north and south. Only a few communities that Jeff knows of have these ideal landscape configurations: Sedona in Arizona, Santa Barbara on the California coast, and Woodstock in the Catskills.

People may not be able to explain why they find Woodstock so appealing, but they're experiencing the forces of the landscape as accounted for by feng shui. Even if feng shui sounds alien, who could disagree that Woodstock exerts a magical pull with its mixture of mountains and valleys, its gateway location between the Hudson Valley and the Catskills, its blending of a wilderness park and cosmopolitan village life. The only thing missing is employment.

The question Jeff most often heard as supervisor wasn't "Where was the concert held?" but "How do people get to live here? There must be some trick." The answer has never been easy, short of being wealthy upon arrival, perhaps as a "Trustafarian" as Jeff might say. Many Woodstockers are retired, either as weekenders who've settled here full time or as former IBMers who remained after their Ulster facilities closed in the early 1990's, blowing a hole in the local economy.

The median age in Woodstock is 48 but seems much older at town meetings and events. In the past decade the town's population fell by 10 percent to 5,884 residents in the 2010 census. Real estate values, already the highest in the region, have doubled in the past 14 years. So younger people and young families don't find many opportunities. There are only two employers of any size,

Ametek Rotron, which has been here since 1949 and employs 240 people for the manufacturing of fans for commercial and military purposes, and IPA Tools, a family business which took over the former bowling alley in 2010 and has 40 workers who produce tools for professional mechanics.

Many people commute out of town to jobs, an hour to Albany, perhaps, or an hour to Poughkeepsie. Others work at home via the Internet. Some of us who commute between bed and computer never seem to get out of our bathrobes.

The gift shops ride the ups and downs of the seasons and the weather that affects weekend crowds. Some shops have lasted for 20 or 30 years. Other storefronts change every few years. People work as real estate agents, carpenters, or gardeners, finding jobs in the economy created by the second home owners. For a time during the real estate run-up of the mid-2000's, it seemed that Woodstock might become a millionaires' haven, but now the typical couple looking for a weekend retreat is from Brooklyn or Queens, people in their 30's or 40's yearning for rustic downtime. No doubt, many weekenders dream of living here full time, but face the conundrum of giving up careers for the uncertainties of cobbling together an upstate life.

All we can say is take heart. From the start, Woodstockers have been defying the odds. In 1791 and 1792 an agent for the Holland Land Company passed through the Lake Hill area and reported that the "land is dry and unfruitful, produces nothing but oak and chestnut, and is hardly peopled." The land hasn't changed, but people have now been settling here for more than two centuries and establishing lives for themselves. It takes enterprise, fortitude, and a sense of humor. Does that sound like you? If so, welcome.

From glass blowers to boarding house owners, bohemian painters to rock 'n' rollers, party-crazed visitors to Thoreauvian hermits, our little mountain town has been a magnet for some of the best, brightest, and most eccentric characters this country has known. Join us. In a small town dreams can grow surprisingly large.

They Lived in Woodstock...
and Some Still Do

Each generation of newcomers learns about the old Woodstock families, the ones who were here long before the hippies, the bohemian painters, or the summer boarders. Some families who've been here since the decades before and after the Civil War would include the **Reynolds, Van de Bogarts, Wilburs, Bonesteels, Roses, Shultises, Happys, Mowers, MacDaniels, Elwyns,** and **Longyears.**

The first decades of the arts colony brought such painters, sculptors and craftsmen as **Bolton Brown, Birge Harrison, John Carlson, Andrew Dasburg, George Bellows, Eugene Speicher, Konrad Cramer, Henry Lee McFee, Peggy Bacon, Eva Watson-Schutze, Charles Rosen, Leon Kroll, Zulma Steele, Yasuo Kuniyoshi, Gaston Lachaise** and **Alexander Archipenko.**

Among the guests at Byrdcliffe between 1910 and 1940 were feminist author **Charlotte Perkins Gilman;** New Dealer **Harry Hopkins;** educator **John Dewey;** naturalist **John Burroughs;** musicians **Arnold Dometsch, William Kroll,** and **Leon Barzin;** authors **Will Durant, Heinrich Mann,** and **Owen Wister;** journalists **Walter Weyl** and **Heywood Broun;** historian **James Shotwell;** poet **Wallace Stevens;** and dancer **Isadora Duncan.**

Some of **Hervey White's** earliest friends at the

Maverick were musicians who created the Concert Hall series. In the 1920's young artists joined the community, including **Arnold** and **Lucile Blanch**, **Harry Gottlieb**, **Eugenie Gershoy**, **Austin Mecklem**, **Hannah Small**, and **Carl Walters**. They were later joined by **Eugene Ludins** and **John Flannagan**. Later came **Russell** and **Doris Lee** and **Raoul Hague**, a prominent sculptor who lived for almost 50 years in Hervey White's original house.

In the early 1930s **Joseph Campbell** spent several years at the Maverick, consumed by reading while developing his ideas about myths. He collaborated on *A Skeleton Key to Finnegans Wake* with **Henry Morton Robinson**, a longtime Maverick resident who later wrote the bestselling novel of 1950, *The Cardinal*, which was filmed by Otto Preminger. **Philip Guston** first rented a Woodstock studio in 1941, but moved to the Maverick full time in 1967, where he produced his famous late paintings. In the early 1970s his friend **Philip Roth** was a neighbor. Poets **Edna St. Vincent Millay**, **Robert Duncan**, and **Kenneth Patchen** also spent time on the Maverick. As a boy, **Robert De Niro** was sent to stay here, bringing along a rifle and 1,000 rounds of ammunition.

Later generations of Woodstock artists included **Henry Mattson**, **Bruce Currie**, **Fletcher Martin**, **Eduardo Chavez**, and **John Pike**. A few are still alive from the heyday of the 1950's and 1960's, such as **William Pachner**.

Albert Grossman moved to Woodstock in 1964.

He managed some huge stars: **Bob Dylan**, **Peter, Paul, and Mary**, and **Janis Joplin**. In 1965 his assistant introduced Dylan to **The Band**, who became popular local residents. Others whom Grossman brought included the **Paul Butterfield Blues Band**, **Phil Ochs**, **Richie Havens**, **Eric Andersen**, and **Todd Rundgren**, who established his own studio in Mink Hollow. **Jimi Hendrix's** manager brought him to the area. **Van Morrison** spent time on Spencer Road and in the village. **John Sebastian** settled here. Folk musicians came: **Happy Traum** and **Artie Traum**, **Geoff** and **Maria Muldaur**, **Tom Paxton**. The jazz musicians included **Jack DeJohnette**, **Carla Bley**, **Warren Bernhardt**, **Anthony Braxton**, **David Sancious**, **Baikida Carroll**, **Pat Metheny**, and **David Sanborn**. **Orleans** led by **John Hall** had hits in the 1970's. More recent residents include **Kate Pierson** of the B-52s who owns a motel on Route 28.

In 1971 **Peter Mayer** founded Overlook Press with his father in an apple shed on the lower slopes of Overlook Mountain. **Ian** and **Betty Ballantine**, who helped launch paperback publishing by founding Bantam Books and then Ballantine Books, also made Woodstock a home.

NBA basketball coach **Phil Jackson** was in Woodstock in the mid-1970's and the mid-1980's when he coached the Albany Patroons in the Continental Basketball League. **Phillipe Petit**, who walked the highwire between the World Trade Center towers in 1974, lives here today.

Acknowledgments

This *Pocket Guide to Woodstock* is a book of personal impressions and opinions, but not of original historical research. For that we began with Alf Evers's magisterial *Woodstock: History of an American Town* and then dipped into his other books, *The Catskills: From Wilderness to Woodstock* and *In Catskill Country: Collected Essays on Mountain History, Life, and Lore.* Anita M. Smith's *Woodstock History and Hearsay* is a treasure trove. In 1923 Richard Le Gallienne wrote a short town history for a Woodstock Artists Association catalog. Edgar Leaycraft, the former town historian, wrote a concise overview posted at the town's website, woodstockny.org. Richard Heppner, the current town historian, has terrific material at his web site, woodstockhistory.org. Weston Blelock of the Historical Society of Woodstock encouraged this project from the start. JoAnn Margolis, the group's archivist, helped. We particularly liked the Society's Kid's History Club "Talking Houses" project. Carl Van Wagenen shared his unpublished manuscript *Woodstock Then: Woodstock Now*, an amazing feat of recollection and research. Jean Lasher Gaede has compiled a loving scrapbook of memories and clippings, *Woodstock Gatherings: Apple Bites & Ashes.* Janine Fallon-Mower has captured the past in two wonderful collections of old photographs, *Woodstock* and *Woodstock Revisited*, and in her family history, *American Tapestry: The Mowers of Maple Lane, Woodstock, New York.* With Eric Kuntsen she co-authored *A View*

From the Sixth: Woodstock's Golf Club 1929-2004. Who knew that Rube Goldberg played golf?

For rock 'n' rock history, we relied on Michael Lang's *The Road to Woodstock* written with Holly George-Warren. He had three partners in his venture, but we've focused on him as the Woodstocker in the group. Paul Smart's *Rock & Woodstock* is hugely entertaining. *Roots of the 1969 Woodstock Festival: The Backstory to "Woodstock"* edited by Weston Blelock and Julia Blelock provides great background and photos.

William Rhodes's *Ulster County, New York: The Architectural History and Guide* is excellent. *Woodstock's Art Heritage: The Permanent Collection of the Woodstock Arts Association* and *The Maverick: Hervey White's Colony of the Arts* provide fascinating overviews by Tom Wolf. Polly Kline wrote two good short histories: *The Art Students League in Woodstock* and *A Single Purpose: The Study of Art: The History of the Woodstock School of Art.*

For geological information, we thank Robert Titus, who shared his *Woodstock Times* articles as well as his *Kaatskill Life* article about Sloan Gorge. Michael Kudish's *The Catskill Forest: A History* an invaluable resource. So is Mike himself who shared his field notes and observations. Erik Kiviat and Ingrid Haeckel of Hudsonia shared early findings from their habitat survey of town.

The Internet has been a resource. We've used the Ulster Publishing website for *Woodstock Times* articles. Many organizations have posted their own histories on their websites. Wikipedia rarely fails to provide some leads. On YouTube we found excerpts from David McDonald's movie, *Woodstock Revisited*. We found a Woodstock University talk given by Marylou Paturel about the Café Espresso. At Cambiz Khosravi's website we watched his 4'33" video about John Cages's 4'33. Martha Frankel's blog about the Joyous Lake in its heyday was terrific.

Many people took time for interviews and tours: Emily Jones at the Woodstock Artists Association, Matthew Leaycraft at Byrdcliffe, Nancy Campbell at the Woodstock School of Art, Schoan at the Zen Mountain Monastery, Jan Tarlin at KTD, Jenny Brown at the Woodstock Farm Animal Sanctuary, Reverend Josh Bode at the Woodstock Reformed Church, Reverend Sonja Tillberg MacLary at Christ First Lutheran, Emily Lenz at the D. Wigmore Fine Art gallery's "Woodstock Story" show.

And others: Megan Reynolds for Woodstock Farm Festival information, Gay Leonhardt for Woodstock Land Conservancy history, Peter Blum and Michael Berg for Family of Woodstock history, David Corbett for an update on the Comeau trails, Peter Schoenberger for birding advice, Sam Magarelli for his insights into the town's volunteers, Marc Plate for a short course in real estate trends, Meira Blaustein for recapping the Woodstock Film Festival, Elli Michaels for the story behind Bird-on-a-Cliff, Ariel Shanberg for the history of the Center for Photography at Woodstock, Cyrus and Nancy Adler for the background of the Tinker Street Cinema, Jeremy Wilber for his memorable bar stories, and Jeff Moran for feng shui.

We especially want to thank Barry Samuels, Richard Heppner, and Jeremy Wilber for commenting on the manuscript, and Leslie Gerber for proofreading it. Jerry Washington, David Holden, and Alan McKnight gave hours of time to produce the maps.

If we got anything wrong, we apologize. If we got everything right, we sigh with relief. The one thing we've learned for certain about Woodstock's history is that there is always more to be learned.

"Why should we be interested in history? The present is so insistent, so absorbing, so apparently different from the past and so self-sufficient, that the effort to grasp it might be more than enough for our powers," wrote Martin Schutze, the first president of the Woodstock Historical Society, in 1930. His answer then still stands today. "The present is not self-sufficient, except to those who are still enjoying the few privileged years of first love. After these brief years life must become aware of continuity of effort and growth."

The more we'd learned about Woodstock in the past, the deeper our appreciation has become for Woodstock today.

❖ ❖ ❖

About the Authors

Michael Perkins is Program Director for the Woodstock Library Forum. He was Chair of the 1987 Woodstock Bicentennial Celebration, and has led many tours of Woodstock. A poet, novelist, critic, and editor, he is the author of two previous local guidebooks: *The Woodstock*  *Guild and its Byrdcliffe Arts Colony: A Brief Guide* and *The Friends of the Library Guide to Woodstock*.

❖ ❖ ❖

 Will Nixon's poetry books are *My Late Mother as a Ruffed Grouse* and *Love in the City of Grudges,* as well as the chapbooks *When I Had It Made* and *The Fish Are Laughing.*

A former environmental journalist, he was a contributing editor to the *Amicus Journal,* published by the Natural Resources Defense Council, and a special correspondent for the *Adirondack Explorer.* His website and blog are at willnixon.com.

❖ ❖ ❖

Credits

Village building photos by Lisa Van Vertloh.

Other building photos courtesy of the Zen Mountain Monastery, Karma Triyana Dharmachakra, Woodstock School of Art

Historical photos courtesy of the Historical Society of Woodstock, Woodstock Public Library

Alf Evers photo courtesy of Ed Sanders

Overlook Hikers photo courtesy of Diane Sirois

Bearsville stream photo courtesy of Joe Tantillo

Easter Girl photo by Dion Ogust

Michael Perkins author photo by Mikhail Horowitz

Will Nixon author photo by George J. Nicholson

Library girls photo by Lesley Sawhill

Town maps by Alan McKnight

Trail maps by David Holden

CIP by Amy Raff

Praise for **Walking Woodstock:**

Journeys into the Wild Heart of America's Most Famous Small Town

"The Hudson Valley has produced some of the great peregrinations of our time, most notably by John Burroughs, an inveterate walker. Add Michael Perkins and Will Nixon to the list—these are charming essays, some of them with a bit more bite than you'd guess!"

—Bill McKibben, *Wandering Home*

"No more informed, energized, cantankerous and amiable company could be found than these two foot soldiers of field and stream. Let them guide you where they go. And feel free to follow in their footsteps."

—Spider Barbour, *Wild Flora of the Northeast*

"Michael Perkins and Will Nixon walk a lot. They walk everywhere. They play off each other's strengths and weaknesses and together seem to have a blast wandering around exploring the nooks and crannies of the area while debating the world at large...

One of the few books I've read that I was sorry to see end."
—*Kaatskill Life*

"Here is an insider's book of Woodstock trails, with good stories on 'lost roads,' cairns, forgotten history, and above all—walking. If this inspired book doesn't get us up and out and walking, nothing will."
—Gioia Timpanelli, *What Makes a Child Lucky*

"*Walking Woodstock* is the perfect guidebook to America's first alternative religion and her oldest, most venerable revolutionary act. Read it as a natural history of the local flora and fauna (including the human variety), as a record of an evolving friendship between kindred souls, or a personal challenge to wear out your next pair of shoes."
—Clark Strand, *How to Believe in God: Whether You Believe in Religion or Not*

For further information, visit bushwhackbooks.com.